Introducing
the Bible

William Barclay

Introducing the Bible

Revised and updated by
John Rogerson

Foreword by
Ronnie Barclay

ABINGDON PRESS/Nashville

Introducing the Bible
Text copyright © BRF and IBRA 1972
Reprinted (with revised Aids to Reading) 1981

Published jointly by
The Bible Reading Fellowship
and
The International Bible Reading Association
(National Christian Education Council)

First edition 1972
Reprinted 1972, 1977
Reprinted (with revised Aids to Reading) 1981
New edition with Rogerson material was done in 1992.
Abingdon Press edition published in 1997.

The foreword and maps are abridgement for the Abingdon Press edition.
ISBN 978-0-687-36590-6

This book is printed on recycled, acid-free paper.

12 13 14 – 19

MANUFACTURED IN THE UNITED STATES OF AMERICA

Contents

Foreword

*I*NTRODUCING THE BIBLE had great significance in my
father's life. It was written not long after my father had been told that
he had Parkinson's disease and he realized that he must use wisely the
precious years he had left to him to communicate the message he
loved so much. He would have been delighted to see this twenty-fifth
anniversary edition of a book that fulfills one of his most treasured
aims as a writer. He used to say, "My one aim has been to make the
picture of Jesus live again" and this book is a wonderful example of his
skill in making the Scriptures and Jesus meaningful for us. One
enthusiastic reader's response to the book was, "He rolled back the
stone from the tomb of my ignorance, allowing me to ascend to the
threshold of Christian understanding."

"If you want to keep alive, keep learning. . . . To think is a necessity
of the Christian life." My father firmly believed that our faith is
strengthened by study and by a fuller understanding of the message
that the Bible gives us. He does not push his views, but gives each
reader the necessary material to make his or her own faith stronger
through knowledge and learning. "I do not wish to persuade people to
think as I do; I only wish to make them think." My father loved to
tell the story of two famous men discussing a well-known author: "I
don't know why you read his books," said the first man. "You don't

believe a word he says." "No, I don't, but he does!" replied his friend. It is my father's aim to stimulate and challenge you and to help you to grow in your Christian faith.

It is my father's hope and mine that this twenty-fifth edition of *Introducing the Bible* will enable you to understand the Bible better, to love it more, and in it to see Jesus more clearly.

—Ronnie Barclay

Prayers for Bible Study

It was the prayer of the Psalmist:

> *Open my eyes, that I may behold*
> *wondrous things out of thy law (Psalm 119:18).*

O God, our Father,
> *Open our eyes and enlighten our minds,*
>> *as we study your word.*
So grant that
> *our minds may know your truth,*
> *and our hearts may feel your love;*
And then confirm and strengthen our wills,
that we may go out to live what we have learned:
> *through Jesus Christ our Lord,*

Amen.

O God,
> *Help us to study your word,*
>> *not only to know about our blessed Lord,*

> *but also to know him;*
> *not only to learn about him,*
>   *but also to encounter him;*
> *not only to grow in knowledge,*
>   *but also to increase in love;*
> *not only to love him with our hearts,*
>   *but also to obey him with our lives;*
> *So that knowing him, loving him, and obeying him,*
> *we too may say: For me to live is Christ.*
>   *This we ask for your love's sake.*

Amen.

> *O God,*
>   *as we study your word,*
>   *grant us persistence,*
>   *that we may not cease from study,*
>   *until we find its meaning.*
> *Take from us the prejudice,*
>   *which would shut our eyes to the truth.*
> *Never let us love systems*
>   *more than we love you.*
> *And then give us the humility which will accept and obey*
> *what you say to us and what you tell us to do:*
>   *through Jesus Christ our Lord.*
> *Amen.*

> *O God, our Father,*
>   *as we read your word,*
>   *humble us at the sight of your holiness,*
>   *and then comfort us with the memory of your mercy.*
> *Humiliate us with the realization of our sinfulness,*
>   *and then uplift us at the sight of your love.*

Help us in your word
to know our sin
and to find our Savior:
through Jesus Christ our Lord.
Amen.

O God, our Father,
help us in the study of your word to find
guidance for our problems
strength for our temptations;
power for our tasks;
comfort for our sorrows;
your fellowship for our loneliness.
When we are lazy and lethargic,
let your word stimulate us to thought and to action.
When we are restless and distracted,
let your word calm our troubled hearts
with the peace that passes understanding.

In the study of your word, open your hand
and satisfy our every need:
through Jesus Christ our Lord.

Amen.

Introduction

WILLIAM BARCLAY WAS undoubtedly the greatest popular writer on the Bible in Britain in the twentieth century. His *Daily Study Bible,* a scholarly devotional commentary on the whole of the New Testament, has been reprinted many times, and translated into many languages. In addition, he wrote books on the New Testament such as *The Mind of Paul, The Master's Men, Turning to God* and *The Lord's Supper,* not to mention books of prayers, epilogues and Bible Study outlines for young people. *Introducing the Bible* was first published in 1972 and was reprinted three times. It has helped many readers to see that a questioning and positively critical attitude to the Bible, so far from being a hindrance, is in fact a necessity, if the Bible's central message is to be grasped and put into practice.

This was Barclay's great gift. Professionally, he was a New Testament scholar who taught for the whole of his academic career in the University of Glasgow. But he had also been a parish minister in the Church of Scotland, and he never lost his pastoral touch, his desire to place his scholarship at the service of ordinary church members, including young people. In performing this task, he not only drew upon the resources of biblical scholarship, but he also had a phenomenal store of illustrations and stories culled from history, literature, theology and devotional writings. The manner in which he lightened his text with such illustrations and stories contributed to the readability and the power of his writing.

Introducing the Bible is a vintage example of William Barclay's writing, combining as it does his knowledge of the ancient world, his robust Reformation faith, his acceptance of the need for biblical criticism and his desire that people should discover that the Bible is a source of life and hope. In 1990, when the Bible Reading Fellowship was wondering whether to reprint the book or to commission a new work to replace it, it was my own opinion that much of the book was still valuable, and that no writer whom I could think of would be capable of producing anything so successful. It was therefore decided that I should edit *Introducing the Bible,* adding to it an account of the changes in approaching the subject that have occurred in the past twenty years. In the event, I have omitted the first chapter, entitled "The Ancient Book", as well as a number of passages from the subsequent chapters that express views no longer current in biblical scholarship. Readers will still have, however, over ninety percent of the original. In this introduction, I shall place the remainder of the book in the context of recent scholarship.

Original Meaning of Scripture

I begin with Barclay's criticism on page 115 of the use that James Stewart made of Acts 27:29. The Acts passage describes how, during the storm that attended Paul's voyage to Rome, the crew cast out four anchors to keep the ship from drifting on to rocks. Stewart used the passage to describe the four anchors that every believer should have: hope, duty, prayer, and the cross of Christ. Barclay commented that "the use of this method by even so great a preacher cannot justify it for us. It is the original meaning of Scripture that we must set out to find."

Of course, Barclay was right. The starting-point of all biblical interpretation must be the attempt to find what the writer intended: and the writer of Acts had four actual anchors in mind, not four spiritual ones! But I want to qualify what Barclay wrote and put in a word of defense for James Stewart.

It is not as easy to discover the original intention of biblical writers as we might think; and, on certain crucial issues there have been deep differences of opinion among experts, for example, about what Paul means when he says that Christ is the end of the law (Romans 10:4). Again, in Old Testament studies, it has been argued that the original historical or worship circumstances of many psalms have been deliberately obscured during their process of composition precisely so that they can be used by worshippers with quite varying needs or moods. The fact that there are these differences of opinion or uncertainties does not mean that scholars should give up trying to find the original meanings. However, it does mean that we must recognize that our results are not always certain, and that some texts (psalms, for example) may not have "original meanings."

Different Interpretations of the Text

The next point to note is that the meaning of a text cannot be restricted to what its author intended. I discovered this for myself when I read a long review of one of my books, and recognized that the reviewer had understood what the book was about far better than I, the author, had done. The same is true in music, where composers are rarely the best interpreters of their music. In the study of the Bible, this brings us to an important issue that often confuses people. In Isaiah 52:13–53:12, the prophet describes the suffering and death of "a man of sorrows and acquainted with grief." A chorus declares "surely he has borne our griefs and carried our sorrows" and concludes that God has "laid on him the iniquity of us all."

Who is the prophet writing about? Barclay on pages 41-42 refers to some of the theories that have been put forward about the identity of the Suffering Servant and professes not to know the true answer to the question; that is to say, he accepts that we do not know who or what the original writer intended. He then goes on to say that this figure found complete fulfillment in Jesus Christ, and that this was what the New Testament writers also believed. So, did the writer of Isaiah 52:13–53:12 have Jesus in mind when he wrote? Surely not; for to accept this would be to suppose that he was writing something that had nothing to do with his own times and situation, nothing to say to his original hearers or readers, and something that would make no sense to readers for hundreds of years until the time of Christ. The prophets simply did not work like that. As Barclay rightly points out, they were the focus of contact between God and his people, declaring to them what God was doing.

The answer to our question is to be given along the following lines. Isaiah 52:13–53:12 is describing someone who had already died and suffered when the text was written down (note the past tenses: he grew up, he was despised, he was oppressed). That someone, whose identity we cannot determine, had been rejected and had suffered, and after his death his despisers had come to realize that he had been God's chosen instrument. For centuries thereafter, when readers read this passage they thought that it might refer to Jeremiah or to the people of Israel. But, after the death of Jesus, Christians saw the passage through completely new eyes. If the original servant had been one through whose sufferings God had been working out his purposes, this was supremely the case with Jesus, the Suffering Servant *par excellence.* Thus, the passage *can* be understood in relation to the death of Jesus, not because this is what the writer intended, but because the passage's latent meaning becomes apparent when we see it in the light of the death of Jesus. We can affirm both that the writer of Isaiah 52:13–53:12 was not writing about Jesus *and* that it is appropriate for Christians to read the passage with Jesus in mind.

The same is true of Isaiah 7:14. In that verse, Isaiah speaks to King Ahaz of a woman who will bear a child whose name will be "God-with-us" (in Hebrew, *Immanuel).* The prophet, as the context makes clear, is speaking to the king about the immediate future, and we can speculate about the identity of the woman and child from the perspective of the life and times of Isaiah, without arriving at complete certainty. The writers of the New Testament, however, saw in this verse an allusion to the birth of Jesus who is indeed God-with-us, even though Isaiah was referring to a woman and baby of his own times.

We thus see that Barclay's insistence on discovering and sticking to the meaning intended by the biblical writers leaves much unsaid, and this gives us the chance to defend James Stewart's application of the four anchors. Of course the writer of Acts did not intend the anchors to mean hope, duty, prayer and the cross. However, we often liken times of great personal or family difficulty to a storm that threatens to force us on to the rocks, and so it seems to me to be appropriate to speak of spiritual anchors that can help us in times of crisis. Provided that we are honest about what we are doing, and do not make a passage mean the opposite of what we believe its intention to be, we can find it encouraging and exciting to read the Bible creatively and imaginatively. The alternative is to say that only scholars can tell us what the Bible means, and that they have the power of veto over our use of the Bible in preaching, prayer and meditation.

The Importance of the Reader

This brings us to the next topic, which is that of the reader. If we have discovered anything in the years since Barclay wrote *Introducing the Bible,* it is the importance of the reader. What we make of a text will depend upon what we bring to it—which is why I have retained Barclay's "Prayers for Bible Study" at the beginning of the book. Barclay, like myself, was an academic working in a relatively privileged environment. But what happens if the reader is not a British professor but a desperately poor slum-dweller in a large South American city? This is the challenge which liberation theologians have thrown down to Western scholars, and it is a challenge whose validity we must accept. It is the claim that the Bible must be read meaningfully in a given situation if it is to be God's word for its readers.

One of the effects of Liberation Theology has been to highlight passages that most of us have never noticed. How many readers could identify the following verses?

Our inheritance has been turned over to strangers;
  our homes to aliens.
We have become orphans, fatherless;
  our mothers are like widows.

We must pay for the water we drink;
  the wood we get must be bought.
Our skin is black as an oven
  from the scorching heat of famine.
Young men are compelled to grind,
  and boys stagger under loads of wood.

The verses in question are Lamentations 5:2-4, 10, 13, and they are verses that have become important to the destitute and oppressed of South America. Because their plight is mentioned in the Bible, it has given them hope that they are not totally forgotten or worthless.

Another effect of Liberation Theology is to stress interpretations that are in the Bible, but which have been overlooked in the West. The story of Sodom and Gomorrah in Genesis 19 has played an important role in discussions in Western theology about sexual behavior. But Ezekiel 16:49 describes the sin of Sodom in the following words:

This was the guilt of your sister Sodom: she and her daughters had pride, excess of food, and prosperous ease, but did not aid the poor and needy.

How many of us, reading these words, will be able to feel comfortable? As long as we think that the only sin of Sodom was gross sexual immorality (which it was, in Genesis 19) we can feel that we are not condemned as Sodom was. Ezekiel puts the matter in a different light, and it is liberation theologians who have reminded us of the passage and shown how much we have to learn about *what is in the Bible* from readers in situations quite different from our own.

Similar contributions are being made to our understanding of the Bible today from readers who are approaching the Bible with a specific interest in women, or in the problems of the environment. Such approaches have reminded us that, together with material about the Servant of God in Isaiah 40–60, there are important and beautiful passages about the daughter of Sion in Isaiah 52:1-10; 54:1-17; 62:1-12; 66:6-14. Or again, in Genesis 1:26-30, both mankind and animals are commanded to be eaters only of plants and fruit. This vegetarianism is rescinded only in Genesis 9:1-7 after the Flood; and the reason for rescinding it is that mankind is no longer in the image of God as first intended. This is a line of thought with many implications.

It is my belief that Barclay would have agreed with much of what I have written so far. I only worked with him on one occasion, and that was for a few days at the end of September 1965 at the launch of the Old Testament Translator's Translation sponsored by the Bible Society. At the time, he was the author of dozens of best-selling books on the New Testament and Christianity, while I had not quite finished my first year as a new and raw lecturer at Durham. However, I have never forgotten how friendly he was to me, and how, in discussions about how to translate Genesis 1, he responded generously to the suggestions of others present, even when they went against suggestions that he had made. I feel sure that he would have warmed to the thought that oppressed peoples in South America and elsewhere are discovering the living voice of the Bible in their particular situations.

The Bible as Literature

The next matter I wish to address concerns reading the Bible as literature. Let me say at once that I am not suggesting that the Bible is *merely* literature, something in the same bracket as Shakespeare. The point is that the biblical writers, through whose personalities God worked (see Barclay page 155), used literary forms and conventions. If the Bible is the word of God, it is the word of God in literary form, and literary techniques will help us to understand it better. When Barclay wrote *Introducing the Bible,* the application of literary techniques to the interpretation of the Bible was only just beginning. I am therefore describing something that did not exist when Barclay wrote.

A literary reading is primarily interested in the way that narratives are constructed, how characters are presented and what kind of "world" is implied in a text. It is not concerned with discovering what the author of the text intended so much as opening up the text to many possible readings. These interpretations will be valid if they convince other readers that they shed light on the text without distorting its plain meaning.

Take as an example the story of the wedding at Cana in Galilee from John 2:1-11. In this narrative, considered from the point of view of the main characters, we can divide the actors into two groups. On one side are those who are supposed to be in control of the situation but who are not. On the other side are those with no authority or status at the feast, but who are seen to be in control. Those in the first group are the bridegroom, the mother of Jesus and the steward of the feast. The bridegroom is responsible for providing the food and drink, but fails to provide sufficient wine. The mother of Jesus believes that she can resolve the situation by getting Jesus to perform a miracle, but she receives a rebuff ("O woman, what have you to do with me?"). There is irony in the fact that the steward neither knows about the wine running out nor that the new wine had not been provided by the bridegroom.

In the other group are Jesus and the servants. Jesus does indeed rise to the need of the occasion, but in a quite unexpected way. He changes 120 gallons of water into wine, far more than is needed. Are the servants allowed to have some, we wonder? The servants find themselves in possession of knowledge that is denied to the steward of the feast and to the rest of the guests, except the disciples of Jesus. *They* know where the wine has come from, and they have witnessed the glory of Jesus.

This reading of the story has worked entirely with the narrative structure, plot and characterization. We have not asked any historical questions about the location of Cana, the significance of the "third day" on which the feast occurred, the identity of the bridegroom, or why the mother of Jesus, Jesus and the disciples were invited. We have not discussed whether we can accept that Jesus performed the miracle. It is not being suggested that such questions ought not to be asked. It is being suggested that we can look at the narrative purely (but not merely) as a piece of literature and enter its "world."

To read the story in this way suggests a number of thoughts. An observer at the feast would have seen only what the chief steward saw, and would also have praised the bridegroom. This prompts us to ask whether we really know what is going on when we look at, and interpret, the world around us. Are the people who are supposed to be in control of daily affairs, and who think that they are in control, really in control? In the story, Jesus works in secret and only the servants and the disciples know what is really happening. This "hiddenness" in relation to the ways of God in human affairs prompts us to try to see events in the light of God's purposes, and not in terms of the human control of events.

One of the most important things about the "world" of the biblical text, when we enter it in the way described above, is that it contradicts and challenges our own world. Had we been at the feast, we would have regarded the bridegroom and the bride as the happiest people present, and the steward as the most important person present. The story as I have read it sees things quite differently. It is the servants who are the most fortunate, because they see the glory of Jesus, and know where the wine has come from. The most important person at the feast is Jesus for whose work another, the bridegroom, gets all the credit.

This story is not alone in challenging the way our world evaluates things. Jesus told parables that shocked his audience and which can still shock us, if we are open to that possibility. The Good Samaritan was a man from a race greatly disliked by Jews in the first century. In the vineyard, those who worked one hour were paid the same as those who had worked twelve (Matthew 20:1-16). In the story of the two sons, the faithful, elder brother finished up worse off than the wayward, spendthrift, younger brother (Luke 15:11-32). Jesus commended the unjust steward (Luke 16:1-9).

It is true that we do not need literary approaches to the Bible to show us that some stories are provocative when read in the light of our own values. Literary approaches will, however, make us aware of how much the Bible challenges our own world, something that should not really surprise us when we remember that the Bible is addressed to a human race that believes (wrongly) that it can run the world without God and without his laws. In a book entitled *Poetry with a Purpose,*

Harold Fisch, a Jewish biblical scholar and professor of literature, has shown how time and again the literature of the Bible cannot quite be fitted into the categories that have been invented to describe other literature. The Bible does not fit into any of the preconceived ideas and stereotypes that we have about it. It does not fit in because it is not like any other book, and it contains a message that challenges human assumptions.

In the further reading, I have listed some books that amplify the points made in the above paragraphs.

The Letter to the Ephesians

I have two final points to make in conclusion, one very short, the other somewhat longer. On pages 158–59 Barclay attributes the letter to the Ephesians to Paul, and uses this in his discussion about Paul's views of marriage. The current opinion of scholars is that Ephesians was not written by Paul, but by a disciple or admirer of Paul. This is not a view shared by *every* scholar, but it is sufficiently widely accepted to mean that we must read Barclay's comments with a certain amount of reserve.

The Old Testament as "Developing Revelation"

The last, and longer point, concerns Barclay's attitude to the Old Testament. Barclay was not an Old Testament expert, but his views in *Introducing the Bible* reflected an agreement of opinion among Old Testament scholars in the 1970s. Since then, attitudes have changed. On pages 126–27 Barclay invokes the idea of *developing revelation,* and says that God was only able to reveal himself as human capacity developed to receive the revelation. But this is not how the Old Testament views the matter. In the Old Testament, the great figures of faith, Abraham, Moses, David, come at the beginning of biblical history, and the story of Israel is a story of failure and ruined opportunities thereafter. It is true that in the nineteenth and twentieth centuries scholars have reconstructed a history of Israelite religion which suggests that the developed religion of Israel emerged late in its history, and was not already fully fledged in the time of Moses. But this raises a crucial question: Where does God reveal himself? Is it in the history of Israelite religion as reconstructed by scholars or is it in the history of Israel as narrated in the Bible? The answer is that it is in the latter, and this for a simple reason. The Old Testament is a work of prophecy in the broadest sense of the term (see Barclay pages 36–37). It is a prophetic interpretation of the events of Israel's history, in which God is revealed in the way in which the events are narrated. This, again, is why literary approaches to biblical narratives are so important. Scholarly reconstructions of Israelite history are valid projects which should certainly be undertaken; but they can never become a substitute for the Old Testament's interpretation of Israel's history. Barclay made the mistake of thinking that they could, and that the Old Testament was evidence for the evolution of Israel's understanding of God.

The Old Testament as Preparation for the New Testament

We now turn to Barclay's assertions that the Old Testament is an essential stage on the way to Christianity, and that the criterion for finding the word of God in the Old Testament is that it should point to Christ. That the Old Testament is completed by the New, and that without Christ the Old Testament is unfinished, are statements that I affirm. However, we have to determine the implications carefully.

If the Old Testament is fulfilled by the New, this does not mean that it is merely preparation for the New Testament. Consider Psalm 51. There is nothing in the New Testament to match it as a confession of sin. Consider Psalm 103. There is nothing to match it as a joyful hymn of praise to God, our Father, who forgives our sins (we sing a metrical version of it in the hymn "Praise, my soul, the king of heaven"). Consider the book of Job. There is nothing in the New Testament to match it as an exploration of the problems of doubt and of innocent suffering.

Consider the Song of Songs. There is nothing in the New Testament to match this exuberant celebration of the beauty of pure and untrammelled love between a man and a woman. I could go on in this vein.

All these examples give the lie to the idea that we must read the Old Testament in the light of the coming of Jesus. The truth is that we do not need to read the Old Testament in order to find Christ there; we simply need to read the Old Testament as Christians, that is, as people who know that Christ *has* come. It is like an architect who plans a whole site with several buildings. After the first building has been built, we can enjoy it in its own right. When the subsequent buildings are finished we can see the first in the light of the whole conception, but this does not mean that we may not appreciate the construction of the first building and its finer points in its own right.

We can put the matter another way. When God gives himself in love to Israel in the Old Testament, he does not hold back any of his giving. He gives himself fully, even if Israel does not know him as Father, Son and Spirit, and their understanding is affected (as ours is) by sin. Thus, when we read the Old Testament, we see God giving himself fully to his people in love, judgment and suffering. As Christians, we believe that God gave himself fully in becoming human in Jesus Christ. This belief is thus the general context in which we see God giving himself to his people in the Old Testament, and we can read the narratives accordingly. The loss of the Old Testament from the Christian Church in the present century has been a serious occurrence, and I hope that what I have written here will encourage readers to discover a few of the treasures which the Old Testament contains.

Professor John W. Rogerson
Head of the Department of Biblical Studies
University of Sheffield

1.

The Making of the Old Testament

The Canon of Scripture

WE ARE GOING to begin by studying how the Bible was built up and came into being. To put it in technical language, we are going to study the formation of the *canon* of Scripture. The canon of Scripture is that list of books which have been accepted as the Christian Church's written rule of faith; it is the list of the "official" books of the Church; it is the list of books which the Church regards as authoritative and determinative for the story of its own history, and for the formation of its life and doctrine.

A list in this sense and usage contains books *which have had something done to them;* they have been put on the list; but these same books *do something to everything else;* they become the standard by which all other things are judged. So the canon of Scripture was formulated by the Church; in this sense it was not the Bible which made the Church, it was the Church which made the Bible; for the Church existed long before the Bible existed. The early Church did not possess the New Testament; it was busy writing it. On the other hand these books are not merely books which have had the passive experience of having had something done to them; they are books which have the active power of guiding and directing the life and work of the Church.

So we go on to study how there came into being that list of books which the Church accepted as authoritative and which became the basic documents of the Christian faith.

Papyrus and Parchment

If we go into a shop nowadays, and ask for a copy of the Bible, we will be handed one single volume, one book. But if we open that book we will find lists of the books of the Old Testament and of the New Testament. We will find that by the usual reckoning there are 39 books in the Old Testament and 27 in the New Testament, a total of 66 books. This is to say that, when we buy a one-volume Bible, we are really buying a library between two covers. When we go on to investigate this portable library a little more closely, we will find that the writing of it was spread over at least one thousand years, and that its books were written all over the ancient world from distant Babylon to Rome.

If we had lived in biblical times, we would never have made the mistake of thinking of the Bible as one book, because we would never have seen it in the form of one book; it did not exist in that form. In the ancient world literary works were written on rolls. The book form, called the *codex*, did not emerge until round about the second century AD. The Old Testament books were written on skins. The New Testament books were originally written on papyrus. Papyrus was made from the papyrus reed, which grew almost exclusively on the banks of the Nile. It is a bulrush. It can be taller than a man, and thicker than a man's wrist. The pith was cut into long strips; it was then laid down vertically and another row of strips was applied horizontally. It was then moistened; pressure was applied; and there emerged a substance rather like brown paper, after the papyrus had been smoothed off with pumice stone. *Biblos* or *bulbos* is the Greek word from which our word *bible* comes. *Biblos* originally was the word for the papyrus bulrush itself; it then became the word for the papyrus writing material made from that bulrush; it then went on to mean a roll of papyrus; and finally it came to mean a book.

Papyrus was not a cheap material. It was made in sheets which measured about ten by eight inches (25.5cm by 20.5cm). It cost any-thing from two pence a sheet for the cheapest quality to about nine pence for the best quality, and these prices have to be evaluated in the light of the fact that a working-man's wage was four pence a day. The sheets were joined edge to edge to form a long strip of papyrus. A wooden roller was placed at each end. The roll was unrolled with the one hand, and rolled up again with the other as it was read. The writing was in narrow columns, two and a half to three inches (2.5–3.5cm) wide.

There is an overlap period when the roll was vanishing and when the book or codex form was coming into use, during which the codex too was made of papyrus. But usually the codex is made of vellum or parch-ment. Vellum was originally made of calves' skin. *Vitulina charta* it was called and from that phrase the word *vellum* is derived. Its greatest cen-ter of manufacture was Pergamum and it was also called *Pergamênê charta* from which the word *parchment* is derived.

Parchment and papyrus have one advantage—they are both extremely durable. But the whole situation in the ancient world had two disadvantages:

• The roll was unwieldy to use. The result is that the maximum length of roll for all practical purposes was thirty feet (9.14m), and it would take a roll of almost exactly that size to hold the Gospel of Luke or of Matthew, or the book of Acts. This is why no one in the ancient world would ever think of the Old Testa-ment or the New Testament as one book. To such a person the Old and New Testaments would be quite extensive collections of rolls. Even when the codex came in, ancient binding was such that three or four volumes would be needed for even the New Tes-tament. The fact that the Bible is a library would not be lost sight of in the ancient world.

• The other disadvantage was expense, both of the papyrus material itself and of the cost of copying.

The unit of measurement for copying was the *stichos* (plural, *stichoi*). A *stichos* was not a line; to pay by the line would not be satisfactory, for different writers might well get a very different number of words into a line. A *stichos* was the average length of one of Homer's hexameter lines which is sixteen syllables. Books were reckoned in *stichoi*. There is a sixth century New Testament manuscript, Codex Claromontanus, which gives the number of *stichoi* in each book. For example, there are 2,900 *stichoi* in Luke, 2,600 in Matthew, 1,040 in Romans, 251 in Colossians, 20 in 2 John, 2,600 in Acts, 1,200 in the Revelation. In the time of Diocletian (AD 287–305) a price-fixing edict was issued, and the cost of copying was 20 to 25 *denarii* per hundred *stichoi*. A *denarius* was about four pence (in 1972); so this means it cost about a pound to copy one hundred lines, which means that Matthew itself, apart from the papyrus, would cost about £26. This expense was something which remained until printing arrived. There were few who could own a Bible; and until the printed book emerged the Bible rarely existed in one volume.

The Jewish Old Testament

Let us now move on to see the process by which the divine library of the Old Testament came into being and grew up into completeness.

The Jews divided their sacred writings into three sections—the Law, the Prophets and the Writings. This classification goes back to about 180 BC. Jesus the son of Sirach had written a book of wisdom which we now commonly call *Ecclesiasticus*. It was originally written in Hebrew. In the year 132 BC his grandson, thinking it a valuable book and a book deserving to be widely known, while he was staying in Egypt translated it into Greek, and in the Prologue he refers to the teachings of the Law, the Prophets and the others who followed them. He speaks again of the Law, the Prophets and "the other books of our fathers."

The Law consists of the first five books of the Old Testament—Genesis, Exodus, Leviticus, Numbers, Deuteronomy. This section of the Bible is commonly known as the *Pentateuch*, which is a Greek word, meaning the five rolls.

The Prophets came to be divided into two sections. First, there are the Former Prophets. These are the books of Joshua, Judges,

Samuel and Kings. These were reckoned as four books, 1 and 2 Samuel and 1 and 2 Kings, each being reckoned as one book. We usually look on these books as historical books, but the Jews looked on them as prophetic, partly because they tell the story of the great prophets like Elijah and Elisha. Second, there were the Latter Prophets. These were Isaiah, Jeremiah, Ezekiel and the Twelve. We call the Twelve the Minor Prophets—Hosea, Joel, Amos, Obadiah, Jonah, Micah, Nahum, Habakkuk, Zephaniah, Haggai, Zechariah, Malachi. They are not *minor* in the sense that they are in any way lesser or inferior; they are *minor* only in the sense that they are *shorter* than the first three. The Latter Prophets are also reckoned as four books, because the Twelve are reckoned as one.

The Writings are a miscellaneous collection. They are variously classified. One classification is, first, three books of poetry—Psalms, Proverbs, Job; second, the five *megilloth (megillah* means a roll); each of them was connected specially with some great Jewish festival. The Song of Solomon, allegorized to make it speak of the deliverance from Egypt, was associated with the Passover, and was read on the eighth day of the Passover celebrations. Ruth was connected with Pentecost, Because it was a harvest idyll, and Pentecost was the harvest feast; it was read on the second day of Pentecost. Lamentations was read on 9th Ab, which is the anniversary of the destruction of Solomon's temple. Ecclesiastes was read on the third day of the Feast of Tabernacles. Tabernacles commemorated the journey through the wilderness, and during it for a week the people left their houses and lived out of doors in booths made of branches. Ecclesiastes was read to remind men to remember God in the midst of material blessings. Esther was read at the Feast of Purim, for which it provides the reason and the warrant. The five *megilloth* were the only books of the Writings to be read in the Synagogue, and they were read only on the occasions with which they were specially connected. Third, there was one book of prophecy—Daniel. Finally, there were two books of history—Ezra-Nehemiah, counting as one, and Chronicles.

The Jews often counted these books as twenty-four. This number was arrived at by reckoning:

- five books of the Law;
- four books of the Former Prophets, 1 and 2 Samuel and 1 and 2 Kings each being reckoned as one book;
- four books of the Latter Prophets, the Twelve being reckoned as one book;
- eleven books of the Writings, Ezra and Nehemiah, and 1 and 2 Chronicles each being reckoned as one book.

So then let us see how and when each of these three parts of the Old Testament acquired the character of Scripture.

The Law

For the Jew the Law was, and is, the most important thing in the world, the center of the Synagogue service, and the essence of all true religion. The word Law is not quite an adequate title for it; the word Law is in English too legalistic to describe the Jewish Law. There is much more in it and to it than rules and regulations, prohibitions and commands. The Hebrew word is *Torah,* and it means instruction rather than law. The Torah is God's instruction to men and women, by obeying which they find life in this world and life in the world to come. They held that the Law had been created before the creation of the world itself, and that God had looked into the Law and then created the world. When the Kingdom of God fully came, the prophets and the writings would pass away, but the Law would last for ever.

It was held to have been delivered to Moses verbatim and entire by the very hand of God himself. It was even held that God began each day by himself setting time apart to study the Law. The aim was that Jewish children should have the Law "graven on their souls." From their infancy they were instructed in the Law, and many a Jew died rather than be false to the Law which was nothing less than the word of God. Center of everything was the Law, and even the rest of Scripture, great as it was, was no more than commentary on the Law. The center of the Synagogue service was the reading of the Law. It was read one verse at a time in Hebrew, and translated into whatever language the congregation understood. How then did it reach its exalted position? In what follows we try to reconstruct the situation. This is a reconstruction and not a certainty; but it does fit the facts, and the majority of Old Testament scholars would agree with it.

In regard to the Law we have one date from which we can start, and a dramatic start it is. Religion in Judah had been in a sorry state. The good king Hezekiah (*c.* 728–699 BC) had been followed by Manasseh and Amon, who were little better than heathen (2 Kings 21). Their combined reigns lasted for more than half a century, and religion was at its lowest ebb. Then in 621 BC the young Josiah came to the throne. And Josiah "did that which was right in the eyes of the Lord." One of the things he did was to initiate the repair and the restoration of the neglected temple; and during that work the book of the Law was found by Hilkiah in the house of the Lord. The reading of that book of the Law moved the king and the people to repentance and reformation, and that book of the Law became for them the very word of God (2 Kings 22 and 23). There is little doubt what that book was. It was a large part of the book of Deuteronomy. Someone who was at once prophet and priest wrote it in the dark days of Manasseh and Amon, when it was impossible to speak openly, and then hid it in the temple, to be found in due time.

Here is the beginning of the whole movement; here is the first time that part of a book is, so to speak, canonized, and becomes the word of God to God's people. There were other statements of the Law and they too were recovered and collected and cherished. There was the oldest statement of all about the Law, commonly called the little book of the covenant, in Exodus 34. There was the book of the covenant itself, the conditions to which the people of God agreed, when God took them as his people and promised to be their God. This is found in Exodus 20:22–23:33, and in its present form dates back to 900 BC. Then in the middle of the sixth century BC another great section was added. The very essence of Judaism is in the phrase: "You shall be holy, for I the LORD your God am holy" (Leviticus 19:2). So there arose what is called the Holiness Code. The word *holy* here really means *different*. God is the supremely different one, as he has been called, The Wholly Other. His people too are to be different; they are not to live like other nations; they are to accept the fact that they are a people destined to be different. And the life of difference they are to lead is summed up in the Holiness Code in Leviticus 17 to 26. So we have the great sections of the Law, the voice of God coming ever more fully and directly to his people—the ancient little book of the covenant, and the book of the covenant itself, the major part of the book of Deuteronomy, and the Code of Holiness. Slowly the Law is building up. It is of the greatest importance to remember one fact that is emerging. People did not sit down and write a book with the intention of writing a book of Scripture. The books which became Scripture had for years and centuries been the help and the strength of the people. These books had already proved themselves over the centuries to be nothing less than the word of God. They were books which by their own proven value had established their right to be recognized as God's word to men and women. These books which became Scripture were not new books; they were books which time had already proved.

The Making of the Pentateuch

But there is more in the Pentateuch than laws and instruction. The law material in the Pentateuch stands in the context of a narrative which takes the story from the creation of the world to the entry into the Promised Land, and within this narrative there are certain very interesting phenomena. When we study this material, it becomes clear that it is composite and that it comes from more than one source.

Traditionally, it is the work of Moses, but it soon becomes clear that more than Moses had a hand in it. In Genesis there is a list of the kings of Edom, and then there is the sentence, "These are the kings who reigned in the land of Edom, before any king reigned over the Israelites" (Genesis 36:31). The first of the kings is Saul, and Saul is three centuries after Moses, so Moses could hardly have spoken of kings reigning over the Israelites. Genesis 14:14 tells of Abraham's pursuit of his enemies *as far as Dan*. But Dan did not get its name until the time of the Judges (Judges 18:29) after the time of Moses. In Genesis (21:34; 26:14-18) the Philistines are mentioned, but in fact the Philistines did not appear on the scene of history until about 1200 BC, again after the time of Moses. And, above all in this connection, Deuteronomy 34:1-8 tells of the death of Moses, and it is hardly likely that Moses told the story of his own death!

Unquestionably, Moses was the great law-giver of Israel, but equally unquestionably more than his hand is to be seen in the first five books of the Old Testament. There is more than one narrative here and there is more than one author here.

There are other signs that the narrative is composite. Often there are two accounts of the same event. There are two stories about how Beersheba got its name, one connected with Abraham and one connected with Isaac (Genesis 21:31; 26:31). There are two stories of how Bethel got its name, one telling how Jacob gave it its name on the way to Paddan-aram, the other telling how he gave it its name on the way back from Paddan-aram (Genesis 28:19; 35:15). There are two accounts of the banishment of Hagar and Ishmael, in one of which Hagar is banished *before* the child is born (Genesis 16:6-16), and in the other of which she is banished *after* the child is born (Genesis 21:9-21).

There are two versions of the Creation story. In the one, man is created at the end of the whole process of creation, after the sea and the land and the growing things and the beasts and the birds have been created, and in this version man and woman are created at the same time (Genesis 1). In the other, man is created at the beginning of the process; then the garden is created; then the beasts and the birds are formed; then woman is made out of the rib taken from man (Genesis 2). Two stories of the ark in the days of the Flood are interwoven. In the one story the animals are to go into the ark in seven pairs of each; in the other story they are to go in in single pairs (Genesis 7:2, 3; 7:8, 9). All over the narrative it can be seen that two versions, two sources, two accounts are being put together.

Now in this compilation there are times when something else is seen. In Hebrew there are two words for God. There is the word *elôhim,* and there is the name Jahweh or Yahweh. This latter is very interesting and very important; it is the same word as the word Jehovah, which is its much commoner form. In Hebrew there are no vowels in the original script, only consonants, and it was only later that little signs for the vowels were put below the consonants to show what the right pronunciation was. The name of God is represented by the four consonants YHWH. The Jews would never pronounce these four letters as they really sounded; the name of God was too sacred even to be said. Now there was another word, Adonai, which means Lord; and what the Jews did was to take the vowels of the word Adonai and to attach them to the sacred letters YHWH, and from that they got the form Jehovah. Jehovah is really the letters YHWH spelled with the vowels of the word for Lord, but the real form is Jahweh (Yahweh), which was too sacred and too holy to say.

In our English translations of the Old Testament, *elôhim* is translated simply God; but YHWH is translated LORD and is printed in special capital letters, as for instance in Genesis 2:4, 5. This way of printing LORD for Jahweh, or Jehovah, is used in the Authorized Version, the Revised Standard Version, the New English Bible, the New Revised Standard Version and the Revised English Bible. Now when we examine these early books carefully we find that in some sections God is called *elôhim*, God, and in some sections he is called Jahweh, LORD. For instance, right at the beginning of the Bible, in the first Creation story God is called *elôhim*, God (Genesis 1:1–2:3), whereas in the second Creation story God is called Jahweh *elôhim*, LORD God (Genesis 2:4-24). We saw that in the ark story at the Flood there is one version of the story in which the animals are taken in in seven pairs and another in which the animals are taken in in single pairs. In the version in which the animals are taken in in seven pairs the command is given by the LORD, Jahweh (Genesis 7:1, 2); in the version in which the animals go in in single pairs the command is given by God, *elôhim* (Genesis 7:9). So we find that in the very early parts of the Bible there are two interwoven sources, in one of which God is called *elôhim*, and in the other of which he is called Jahweh; that is to say in one source God is called God, and in the other he is called LORD. After a time both sources call God Jahweh, LORD, for in the source which began by calling God *elôhim*, God, we find the famous story of how Moses discovered that the name of

God is Jahweh, the One who is (Exodus 3:13-16), for this was the lesson that Moses received in the mysterious incident of the burning bush (Exodus 3:1-6).

What becomes clear is that the Law, the Pentateuch, did not spring into being ready-made. It is the product of the centuries. It is the essence and the distillation of the voice of God to men and women both in words and in events over the years. Here is the concentrated voice of God over the centuries—first the little book of the covenant; then the larger book of the covenant; then Deuteronomy; then the Holiness Code; then the story of the ways of God compiled by the two different writers; then its molding and interweaving into one, with that complete honesty which would omit nothing and change nothing; until in the end there emerged that wonderful amalgam of law and history which to the Jew was and is the word of God as is nothing else on earth.

The Law as Scripture

But there remains one question still to ask. When did the Law stop being simply a wonderful book, and when did it become Scripture? When did it stop being only a book and become a Bible? This is to ask, when did the oldest part of the Bible begin to be regarded as definitely the word of God? There are three indications to help us to fix a date.

- One of the great dates was the date when the Old Testament was translated into Greek. We shall tell the story of that translation later (see pages 87–89). At the present moment we are concerned only with the date when the Septuagint, as the Greek translation of the Old Testament is called, came into being. It is obviously a great date. When the Old Testament remained in Hebrew its sphere was strictly limited to the Jews; when it was translated into Greek it became the possession of the world. The Old Testament was translated into Greek in the reign of Ptolemy the Second, called Philadelphus, in Egypt, and this Ptolemy reigned from 285 until 246 BC. At first, it was only the Law which was translated, for it was the Law above all which was Scripture for the Jew by that time.

We can therefore begin by saying that the Law was certainly Scripture by about 270 BC. Can we trace it further back?

- The Samaritans even to the present day accept only the Law, the Pentateuch, as Scripture; they do not so accept the rest of the Old Testament. This will mean that they had split from the rest of the nation when the Law had become Scripture, but the rest of the Old Testament had not. The Samaritan split dates to about 350 BC. Therefore away back in 350 BC the Law was already regarded as the word of God.

- When we read Nehemiah 8–10 we find Ezra the scribe reading "the book of the Law" to the people, and the people taking it as the Law of God and the law of their lives. This happened after they had returned from exile. From then on the Jews were to be for ever the people of the Book, and that book the book of the Law. And that happened about 450 BC.

Everything points to the fact that the Law became Scripture, the Law was established as the word of God, around four hundred years before Jesus came into the world as a man. We may take it that the Law, the Pentateuch, the first five books of the Old Testament, has been regarded as Scripture since 400 BC. For very nearly 2,400 years men have found the word of God in the books of the Law. And there is something unique about a book by which men and women have guided their lives not only for hundreds but for thousands of years.

The Prophets

It will be remembered that we began the story of the formation of the Old Testament by seeing that the Jews divided it into three sections—the Law, the Prophets and the Writings. We have now seen how the Law was built up and how by around 400 BC it had become Scripture, and now we turn our attention to the Prophets.

As we have seen, to the Jew the Law was incomparably the greatest part of Scripture; for most modern students of the Bible the Prophets would stand higher than the Law. They would indeed, with the exception of the Psalms, be the most precious part of the Old Testament for most of us. Let us see then how they too became part of the word of God.

We have already seen that the Prophets were divided into two sections—the Former Prophets, and the Latter Prophets. The Former Prophets consist of the books of Joshua, Judges, Samuel and Kings. The authors of these books are completely unknown. There are not even any traditional titles ascribed to them as the books of the Law are all ascribed to Moses. But Jewish tradition did say that Joshua wrote the book of Joshua, that Samuel wrote the books of Judges and Samuel and that Jeremiah wrote the books of Kings. These four books, as the Jews reckoned them, were completed in the sixth and the fifth centuries BC.

It may seem strange to us to find what we regard as history books ranked among the prophetic books. There are two reasons for this. These books tell of the great prophets who functioned before the literary prophets emerged, the non-literary prophets like Samuel and Nathan and Elijah and Elisha. They certainly had prophetic material in them. Second, the Jews took history very seriously. For them the events of history were God in action; history for them was the arena of the activity of God. God, for them, was speaking in events. The events of history were, for them, the demonstration of the truth of the prophetic message. History, too, was for them the voice of God. History for them was the voice of God proclaiming across the centuries that it is well with the good, and it is disaster for the wicked. It was perfectly natural to look on history as prophetic, for history was for them the manifestation of the rule of God (see also page 40).

When we come to the Latter Prophets, the great named prophets, it is well to have a time scheme in our minds as we read them, and to know the events of history which were the background of their writings.

First of them to come, in the latter half of the eighth century, were Amos and Micah. They were writing near the days when the Assyrians invaded Palestine and when the Kingdom of Samaria was wiped out for ever in 722 BC. These two prophets strike the note which is from beginning to end the center of the prophetic message. That message is summed up in a famous phrase—it was the proclamation of *ethical monotheism.* Let us take the second word first, the word *monotheism.* There are three forms of human belief in God. First, there is *polytheism. Polloi* is the Greek for *many; theos* is the Greek for God or a god; and *polytheism* is the word which describes a religion which has many gods. This was the way of the early Greek and Roman religions with Zeus and Apollo and Athene and Aphrodite and all the rest of them. This is the stage of many gods. Second, there is *henotheism.* At this stage people still believe in many gods, but they had come to believe that only one of these gods was valid for them. Each country had its own god, and beyond that country the writ of that god did not run. So each country had its own god, but no one denied that the gods of the other countries were equally real and in their own sphere equally powerful. So Jephthah says to the Ammonites: "Should you not possess what your god Chemosh gives you to possess? And should we not be the ones to possess everything that the LORD [Jahweh] our God has conquered for our benefit?" (Judges 11:24). At this stage Jahweh was the only God for the Hebrews, but that did not mean that Chemosh was not real enough for the Ammonites. At this stage a nation had its own god, and for them that god was the only god, but there was no denial of the rights of other gods in regard to other nations. Lastly, there is the belief in *monotheism,* which is the belief that there is only one God, who is the God of all, the God of this universe and of any other universe that does exist or ever will exist.

This was the first message of the Prophets, the message that there is one God and one God only, to whom Israel must be true. Nor was this altogether easy. In the days when it was believed that each country had its own god, then when people came to stay in a strange country they brought, as it were, their own god with them and built a shrine for him. This is what happened in the case of Solomon. In the days of Solomon Israel was politically a great nation. This led to foreign alliances. Very often a foreign alliance was cemented by the king of the one country marrying the daughter of the king of the other. This is exactly what Solomon did, and these foreign princesses brought their own gods and goddesses with them and so infected the true religion with false faiths (1 Kings 11:1-8). To us monotheism is the only natural belief; in the days of the prophets it was a great discovery, and the prophets were the guardians of it.

Not only did these great early prophets teach monotheism; they also taught *ethical* monotheism. Nowadays religion and morality go hand in hand. But strangely in the ancient days religion and immorality were apt to go hand in hand. Take three instances of this. In the ancient world, when a man founded a new city, it was the custom to lay the foundations of it, and to fix the gateposts of it, in the body of his slaughtered and sacrificed son (1 Kings 16:34). In the worship of the god Molech little children were sacrificed in the fire (2 Kings 23:10). The worship of Baal was the worship of the fertility cult. The Baals were the powers who made the corn grow, and the grapes ripen. The greatest fertility force of all is sex. So to the temples of the Baals there were attached many sacred priestesses who were nothing other than sacred prostitutes, and to have sexual intercourse with one of them was an act of worship. These so-called priestesses were the cult-prostitutes whom Hosea condemns (Hosea 4:14). The prophets had to teach that the most elaborate ritual in the world is no substitute for personal chastity, for social justice, and for love for others and love for God. The whole book of Amos has been called "a cry for social justice," and no text in the Bible is better known than Micah's saying that God does not want sacrifice. What he wants is that men should do justice, and love kindness, and walk humbly with him (Micah 6:6-8). For us these things are part of religion. For the great early prophets they were epoch-making discoveries. The prophets were the great ethical monotheists, insisting that there is one God, and that chastity, mercy and fidelity are the true sacrifices.

Also from the eighth century BC come two more of the great early prophets, and they too have their dominant ideas. As we have seen, the great cry of Amos and Micah is the insistence on social justice. But Hosea is above all the prophet of undefeatable love. Hosea argued from himself to God. Hosea had taken on God's orders a wife from the streets. He treated her with love, but she went back to her old life;

but every time she went back, he took her back again, with a love which would not own defeat. And, so Hosea argued, if I a man can love like that, how much more God?

So we have Amos and Micah with their stress on social justice; and we have Hosea with his stress on love. But there is still another of the great eighth century prophets. The book of Isaiah falls into three pans, and the first part of it—Chapters 1–39—belongs to this same period. Isaiah was an aristocrat and the friend of kings, and he too has his dominant note; and his note is holiness. "Holy, holy, holy is the LORD of hosts" (Isaiah 6:3). Always he confronts men with the holy God. And always he too is insistent that nothing can take the place of justice and of love. Sacrifices, new moons, sabbaths, prayers—by themselves they are without avail.

> *Seek justice,*
> *rescue the oppressed,*
> *defend the orphan,*
> *plead for the widow. (Isaiah 1:17)*

So each of the great eighth-century prophets has his note—Amos and Micah, social justice; Hosea, love; Isaiah, holiness, and it is while remembering their note that we should read them.

In the seventh and the sixth centuries BC there was another group of prophets, proclaiming the word of God in the light of their contemporary history, and always interpreting that history in the light of the purpose of God. In 627 BC Zephaniah saw the Scythian hordes arriving from the East, and saw in that invasion the beginning of the time of judgment for Assyria, and for Moab and for Philistia, and for Judah too. It was for him the warning of the coming of the Day of the Lord. At the same time Nahum was vividly portraying the fall of Nineveh. For a moment it looked as if God was going to strike in history, but the event was the rise of still another great power, the rise of Babylon, and Habakkuk writes wondering at the delay of God, as one tyranny succeeds another.

Then there came two of the greatest of the prophets who both made the discovery which saved Jewish religion from collapse. Jeremiah saw the fall of Jerusalem at the hands of the Babylonians in 586

BC, and Ezekiel lived through the exile with the people in Babylon, where he dreamed of the new order of things which would some day be. But the great contribution of these two was the reminder that religion is not only a national thing; it is a personal thing too.

Now, if you think always in terms of the nation, then if the nation is in the midst of disaster, faith may well collapse; but, if you make the discovery that a man is connected with God, not because he is the member of a nation or a tribe, but because he is a person, then the connection between the individual and God can survive any national trial or disaster. This is exactly what Jeremiah and Ezekiel discovered. They discovered that a man was connected with God, not because he was a Jew, but because he was a man. They discovered personal religion. Like all great discoveries it is a very simple discovery, but few could be more important.

But a new world power was emerging, the power of Persia, and the second section of Isaiah has something of quite extraordinary interest to say about this; the section is Chapters 40 to 55. The leader of the Persians was Cyrus, who had no intention of liberating the Jews from the power of Babylon, and it is very unlikely that Cyrus had ever heard of Jahweh, or would have thought Jahweh of any importance, if he had heard of him. But in spite of that Cyrus has his place in the plan and the purpose of God. God says of Cyrus: "He is my shepherd, and he shall fulfill all my purpose." Cyrus is the anointed whose right hand God has grasped (Isaiah 44:28; 45:1). Cyrus was to be the liberator of the Jews. He did not know it, but he was working out the purposes of God. Here indeed is a philosophy of history. All history is in the hand of God, and even the man who has never heard of God may be, all unknown to himself, the servant of God and the instrument in the hand of God.

It is in this section of Isaiah that we find the picture of the Suffering Servant, that figure who was to have so great an influence on the thought of the New Testament, and almost certainly on the thought of Jesus himself. The picture of the Suffering Servant culminates in Isaiah 53 in the one who was wounded for our transgressions and bruised for our iniquities (Isaiah 53:5). The complete picture of the

Suffering Servant is drawn in what are known as the four Servant Songs (Isaiah 42:1-4; 49:1-6; 50:4-9; 52:13–53:12). It is to be noted that in Isaiah 53 all the verbs up to verse 10 are in the past tense. On the face of it, they are a description of some one whom the prophet knew, and who had suffered, rather than of some one who was to come. It is true that sometimes a prophet was so sure that what he was saying was going to happen that he spoke of it as having already happened, but Isaiah 53 does not read like that.

Who was the sufferer in Isaiah 53? This is one of the questions which has always fascinated and eluded the minds of scholars. In C. R. North's *The Suffering Servant in Deutero-Isaiah* North tells us that S. R. Driver, the great Old Testament scholar, planned to write a commentary on Isaiah, and abandoned the task because of the tangled maze of interpretations in regard to the Servant.

Is the Servant Isaiah himself, who according to Jewish tradition was martyred and buried in a felon's grave, as the Ethiopian thought it might be (Acts 8:34)? Is he Jeremiah, who speaks of himself as "a gentle lamb led to the slaughter" (Jeremiah 11:19)? Is he Jehoiachin, who according to Jewish tradition sacrificed himself to Nebuchadnezzar in order to save the city of Jerusalem from devastation (2 Kings 24:8-20)? Is he Zerubbabel, who after playing a foremost part in the return from exile strangely vanishes from history (Haggai 1:1, 12, 14; 2:21-23; Zechariah 4:6-10)? Or is the Servant the nation of Israel, redemptively suffering for its own sins and the sins of the world? We cannot tell, but we do know beyond a doubt that this figure of the Suffering Servant found its complete fulfillment in Jesus Christ. All over the New Testament Jesus is identified with the Suffering Servant (Acts 3:13; 3:26; 4:27, 30; 8:26-35; Matthew 8:14-17; 12:14-21; Luke 22:37; 2 Corinthians 5:21; 1 Peter 1:19; 2:22-25). No Old Testament figure is so built into the New Testament as the Suffering Servant of Second-Isaiah.

So we have the rise of another world power. Assyria had left the scene and so had Babylon, and now it was the turn of Persia to dominate the stage of history. This was very important for the Jews, for the Persians allowed the Jews to return to Jerusalem, from which the

Babylonians had removed them in exile, so in the late sixth century and in the fifth century we find Haggai and Zechariah urging them on to rebuild the shattered temple, and to try to restore the lost glory.

We find Obadiah condemning Edom because she had stood aside and seen Judah reduced to slavery. We find Joel cheering the people when days were difficult, and Malachi rousing them to new devotion, when devotion had grown cold. In the slackening of devotion the people had come to try to put God off with second-bests, and with the cheapest and the shoddiest things they could offer (Malachi 1:6-14). And in the day of despair and depression Malachi tries to rekindle the flame of devotion in their hearts.

There is one book included among the prophets which we have not yet mentioned—the book of Jonah. This little book is one of the greatest books in the Old Testament, because it calls on the Jews to abandon their exclusiveness, to bring God's word to the Gentiles, to rejoice when the Gentiles accept the message, to believe that even Nineveh can be saved, if Nineveh repents. Jonah is the one supremely missionary book in the Old Testament. It is also one of the latest books for it comes most probably from the fourth century BC.

Prophetic Books as Scripture

We have now to ask when the books of the prophets ceased to be merely precious works of devotional literature and became Scripture.

We have to note regarding the prophets that which we have noted about the other books of the Old Testament. Long before they became Scripture they were known and used and loved. It was because they had proved their power to illuminate the mind and to comfort and strengthen the heart that they did earn a place in Scripture.

It was in the days of the exile that the works of the prophets came to be known and loved. This was so because these books did two things. They foretold the fate of the sinner and of the disobedient and of those who forsook the way of God for their own way. And that part of them had been amply fulfilled. The nation knew only too well now what happened to a nation which disregarded the voice of God. What the prophets had said would happen had happened. But the prophets did not end their message there. Just as they had a message of doom for the disobedient, so they had a message of hope for the penitent. And the Jews had the conviction that just as the message of doom had come true, so the message of hope would also come true. F. C. Grant in his book *How to Read the Bible* (pp. 84, 85) points out that the prophetic message follows a pattern:

(a) Your sins are about to find you out, justice is certain to overtake you—soon;

(b) if God's punishment is severe, he is still concerned with those whom he punishes, and his purpose is to save, not to annihilate;

(c) in this final hour before the stroke of doom, repent!—or, if you repent, God may turn away the threatened punishment and restore you to his favour;

(d) indeed, God, who foresees all things, is aware that a "remnant" will survive, a penitent few, like the living stump of a fallen tree; out of this small handful he will be able to build up once more the nation or the family or the covenant-people of his choice.

In other words, the message of the prophets was compounded in equal parts of threat and promise, of doom and rescue, of the midnight and the dawn. And so the Jews read and studied and drew strength from the prophets in the certainty that, if the prophets had been right about the doom, they would also be right about the restoration. In the darkest days they drew their hope from the prophetic hope.

But these prophetic books drew their special place from another factor in the situation. They were regarded as the great examples of a voice that was now silenced for ever. No longer was there any one to say: "Thus saith the Lord." As the Psalmist said wistfully: "We do not see our emblems; there is no longer any prophet, and there is no one among us who knows how long" (Psalm 74:9). By the time of Zechariah it was true that anyone who claimed to be a prophet was to be regarded as a fraud: "And if any prophets appear again, their fathers and mothers who bore them will say to them, 'You shall not live, for you speak lies in the name of the LORD'; and their fathers and their mothers who bore them shall pierce them through when they prophesy"

(Zechariah 13:3). So in 1 Maccabees it is said: "So there was great distress in Israel, such as had not been since the time that prophets ceased to appear among them" (1 Maccabees 9:27). Simon is made leader and priest, "until a trustworthy prophet should arise" (1 Maccabees 14:41). They will wait until a prophet comes and tells them what to do (1 Maccabees 4:46). There came a time as early as the fourth century BC when the prophets belonged to the splendor of the past; they had spoken with a voice and an accent which was for ever silent. Obviously this gives them a greatness which could never be repeated.

When then did they actually come to be regarded as Scripture? This is something which we can only deduce. In 2 Maccabees 2:13 it is said of Nehemiah that "he also founded a library and collected the books about the kings and prophets, and the writings of David, and letters of kings about votive offerings." It was always part of Jewish tradition that Ezra had a great deal to do with the construction of the collection of Scripture. This is no more than tradition, but it may well be that at that time—about 400 BC—the writings of the prophets were collected and set in order.

But there is one fact which may well give us our due. Daniel is dearly a prophetic book; it is a book which characteristically foretells the future. And yet the strange fact is that in Jewish practice Daniel was never ranked with the Prophets but always with the Writings. This can only mean that Daniel comes from a time when the list of the prophets was closed. If that list had been open, surely Daniel would have been on it. Now the date of Daniel is about 165 BC, and this is an indication that the list of the prophets was probably closed by that time. So it is likely that the prophets came to be regarded as Scripture by round about 200 BC.

The Writings

Slowly the Old Testament is being built up; slowly book after book is gaining admittance, because it could not be denied, and because it bore its inspiration on its face. By about 400 BC the Law was Scripture; and probably by 200 BC the Prophets stood beside the Law. It only remains to see how the Writings won their place.

So then let us turn our attention to these Writings. There were, as we have already noted, eleven of them—Psalms, Proverbs, Job, Ecclesiastes, the Song of Solomon, Ruth, Lamentations, Esther, Ezra-Nehemiah, Chronicles, Daniel. The Writings do not form a unified and homogeneous group like the Law or the Prophets. They are very much a miscellaneous collection, a miscellany, as someone has called them, of independent books. They never quite attained to the place of the other two groups. Some of them had their place on special occasions in the Synagogue worship, but they were not read regularly and systematically at the Synagogue services as the Law and the Prophets were. When the Jews spoke about their Scriptures, they usually spoke about the Law and the Prophets. Jesus said that he had not come to destroy the Law and the Prophets, but to fulfill them (Matthew 5:17). He said that the principle which commands us to do to others as we would have them do to us is the Law and the Prophets (Matthew 7:12). It was the Law and the Prophets which preceded the coming of the Kingdom (Luke 16:16). It was Moses and all the Prophets which Jesus expounded and interpreted on the way to Emmaus (Luke 24:27). It is the Law and the Prophets which are read in the Synagogue (Acts 13:15). If in the New Testament another section is added to Scripture, it is the Law, the Prophets and the Psalms (Luke 24:44).

In the Writings there was something of everything. E. J. Goodspeed in *How Came the Bible?* (p. 39) divides them into philosophical discussion of religion—Job and Ecclesiastes; dirges—Lamentations; love songs—the Song of Solomon; stories—Ruth and Esther; history written from the priestly point of view—Chronicles. F. C. Grant in *How to Read the Bible* (p. 87) distinguishes poetry—Job, Psalms, Song of Solomon, Lamentations; Wisdom books—Ecclesiastes and Proverbs; stories—Esther and Ruth; a prophetic book—Daniel; history—Ezra-Nehemiah and Chronicles. In the Writings we really have the religious literature of a nation, and they won their place, not as a single whole, but piecemeal.

We have first to ask how they got into Scripture at all. We saw that from the fourth century BC onwards it was the conviction of the Jews that the direct voice of God had ceased to speak. Now this would in effect mean that no book written after Ezra had any chance of becoming Scripture. It lay outside the period of direct inspiration. The Rabbis arrived at an odd conclusion about this. If the author of a book was known, and if he was known to have written outside the period of inspiration, then the book did not get into the list of books which were Scripture. That is what kept out Ecclesiasticus, which is one of the very great books, and the omission of which many regret. It was known to be the writing of one Jesus the son of Sirach, who wrote it about 180 BC and whose grandson translated it into Greek about 132 BC. Its date and author were known and therefore it was out. On the other hand, the Rabbis held that if the author of a book was unknown, and if it was a book of sufficient religious value to make it desirable as Scripture, then it was possible to attribute it to one of the great figures who did fall within the period of inspiration. Thus since no one really knew who wrote them, Ruth could be attributed to Samuel; Lamentations to Jeremiah; Proverbs and Ecclesiastes to Solomon; Job to Moses; the Song of Solomon to Solomon, or at least to the time of Hezekiah; all the Psalms to David, although in the middle of the book we find the verse, "The prayers of David son of Jesse are ended" (Psalm 72:20); Ezra and Nehemiah to Ezra. The place that Ezra acquired in Jewish tradition was unique. The Rabbis said: "The Torah was forgotten by Israel, until Ezra went up from Babylon and re-established it," and they also held that, if the Law had not already been given to Moses, Ezra was fit to have received it. To Ezra's place in tradition we will return. It is indeed fortunate that the Jewish Rabbis found a way to preserve these books, for otherwise they might well have vanished.

The Writings as Scripture

We shall now look at the process by which these Writings were established as Scripture, and then after that we shall look at them individually. There are five pieces of evidence which will combine to give us our date.

• We have already had cause to cite what 2 Maccabees 2:13 says about Nehemiah. It says of him that he founded a library and collected the books about the kings and the prophets and the writings of David. If this is to be taken as historical, then we could say that Nehemiah began the collection of the Psalms, and thereby laid the foundation of that section of Scripture which became the Writings.

- We have also referred before to the Prologue which the grandson of Jesus the son of Sirach wrote to his Greek translation of his grandfather's book. In that prologue he refers to the great things handed down—the writings of the Law and the prophets and of others who have followed in their steps. He tells how his grandfather had studied the Law and the Prophets and the books of our fathers. He speaks of the Law and the Prophets and the rest of the books. He never uses the term the Writings, but it is clear that for him there was in addition to the Law and the Prophets a third section of Scripture.

- As we have already noted in Luke 24:44, Jesus is said to have expounded to his disciples after his Resurrection the things about himself in the Law of Moses, the Prophets and the Psalms.

- In the apocryphal book 4 Ezra, called in the printed Apocrypha 2 Esdras, there is a highly colored fictional account of the work of Ezra (Chapter 14). In Ezra's time the Law had been lost, and it was Ezra's divinely appointed task to restore it. He was taken to a field with five men and given a cup of liquid like fire to drink. For forty days and forty nights he dictated non-stop to the five men. During that time ninety-four books were written. Then the Most High said to him: "Make public the twenty-four books that you wrote first and let the worthy and the unworthy read them; but keep the seventy that were written last, in order to give them to the wise among your people." This is obviously legend, but the point is that when this book of 4 Ezra was written in the latter half of the first century AD the Jewish scriptures were composed of twenty-four books, which is the number including the Writings. By that time the Writings were Scripture.

• Round about AD 100 Josephus the Jewish historian laid it down that the Jewish books were fixed and settled, with none to be added and none to be subtracted.

This all fits in, for it is usually held that it was in AD 90 at the Council of Jamnia, near Jaffa, that the Jewish Rabbis finally fixed the contents of Scripture. The Writings were now complete.

When we remember how varied a miscellany the Writings are, we will not be surprised to learn that they did not all become Scripture with the same speed and the same unanimity.

About some of them there never was any question. There was never any question about the Psalms. The Psalms were the hymn-book and the prayer-book of the Temple. They were intimately connected with the worship and the liturgy of the Temple. Each day of the week had its special Psalm with a rabbinic reason to explain its attachment.

Psalm 24 was the Psalm for the first day of the week. "The earth is the Lord's and all that is in it"—this commemorated the first day of creation, "when God possessed the world and ruled in it." Psalm 48 was the Psalm for the second day of the week. "Great is the Lord and greatly to be praised"—because on the second day of creation "God divided his works and reigned over them." Psalm 82 was the Psalm for the third day of the week. "God has taken his place in the divine council"—"because on that day the earth appeared on which are the Judge and the judged." Psalm 94 was the Psalm for the fourth day. "O LORD, thou God of vengeance"—"because on the fourth day God made the sun, moon and stars, and will be avenged on those that worship them." Psalm 81 was the Psalm for the fifth day. "Sing aloud to God our strength"—"because of the variety of creatures created on that day to praise his name." Psalm 93 was the Psalm for the sixth day. "The Lord reigns"—"because on that day God finished his works and made man, and the Lord ruled over all his works." For the seventh day, the Sabbath, the Psalm was Psalm 92. "It is good to give thanks to the LORD"—"because the Sabbath is symbolic of the day, when after the six thousand years dispensation, God will reign over all, and his glory and service will fill the earth with thanksgiving."

Both for public worship and for private devotion the Psalms stood supreme, and never was their right to a place within Scripture challenged.

The five rolls, the *Megilloth*, which were connected with the great festivals and memorials had a secure place, although as we shall see some of them were challenged.

Chronicles, Job, Ezra-Nehemiah and Daniel had a special place, because the high priest read publicly from them on the eve of the greatest of all Jewish religious occasions, the Day of Atonement.

Three books were particularly questioned. The Song of Solomon came under question, because, unless it is read as an allegory, which it was originally never meant to be, it is a passionate love poem of very physical love, indeed one of the supreme love poems of the world. Ecclesiastes came under question because of its weary pessimism. Do your best here, and live your hardest here, is its message, because there is nothing on the other side of death but the land of shadows (Ecclesiastes 9:10). Esther came under question, because, extraordinary as it may seem, the name of God is never mentioned in it from beginning to end, and it is the warrant for the Festival of Purim, which commemorates the victory of Mordecai over Haman, but which is not one of the Festivals laid down in the Law at all.

But after the Council of Jamnia the doubts were stilled and the questions were silenced.

So then, in the guidance and the providence of God the Old Testament reached its present form. And we may well note three things about it.

- It is composed of books, which before they entered the sacred realm of Scripture, had stood the test of the years. It was not that a man wrote a book with the intention of writing a book which should be Scripture. The man wrote his book; he delivered it to the people and to the years. Throughout the years and the centuries men and women came to love that book and to stay their hearts on it, and God used that book for his purposes. And then there came a day when people recognized that that book was nothing less than a message of God. If we liked to do so, we could say that books became Scripture by the principle of the survival of the fittest. A book became part of the Bible because it was so effective and so obviously used by God that none could stop it.

• We must always remember that it took from the eighth century to the second century BC to write the Old Testament. Think of that in terms of modern history. The equivalent would be a book which people began to write in the fourteenth century and finished writing in the twentieth century AD. This is something to which we must return, but it is easy to see the difference in the world between 1300 and 1900. Six hundred years is a long time.

• Further, the establishment of the Old Testament as Scripture began with the finding of part of Deuteronomy in 621 BC and ended with the Council of Jamnia in AD 90. This is to say that it took rather more than seven hundred years to build up the Old Testament to the point when there was a canon of Scripture. The roots of the Old Testament go very deep.

2.

The Making of the
New Testament

*T*HE NEW TESTAMENT as we now possess it consists of twenty-seven books. There are four Gospels, one book of Church history, twenty-one letters and one Apocalypse. The first time we meet the New Testament exactly in this shape is in the year AD 367. The great bishop Athanasius was accustomed at Easter time to send a pastoral letter to his people. In the year AD 367 he decided to deal with the books which it was right and proper for a Christian to read and which the Church approved. He listed them, and for the first time the list contains all the books which make up our New Testament. This is to say that the making of the New Testament took more than three hundred years to complete.

From the beginning of its existence the Christian faith was the faith of a book. Christianity was cradled in Judaism, and Judaism was centered in the Synagogue. In its very earliest days the Christian Church had no intention of breaking away from the ancestral worship of the Jews. We find Peter and John on their way up to pray in the Temple (Acts 3:1). We find that both Stephen and Paul began their career as preachers by debating in the Synagogue (Acts 6:8-10; 9:20, 21). The center of the Synagogue service was the reading of the Scripture. That is what the service existed for. It began with a recital of the creed of

Judaism and with the offering of a series of prayers. It ended with an address by a Rabbi or a distinguished stranger. But right in the middle there came the reading of Scripture, and it was for this that the people had assembled.

When it was no longer possible for the Christians to worship in the Synagogue, when the doors of the Synagogue were closed against them, they took the form of the Synagogue service with them. More than that—they took the book of the Synagogue service with them too. In the early days of the Church the New Testament had not yet been written. It was not the New Testament which produced the Church; it was the Church which produced the New Testament. So, in the beginning, it was the Old Testament which was read every Sunday at the Christian services, and usually it was read in the form of its Greek translation, the Septuagint, which is usually denoted by the letters LXX. So in the first days of the Church it was the Old Testament which was the book of the Church; it was the Old Testament which was quoted and read.

For example, in Peter's sermon at Pentecost (Acts 2:14-40) 10 out of 27 verses are Old Testament quotations—Acts 2:17-21 = Joel 2:28-32; Acts 2:25-28 = Psalm 16:8-11; Acts 2:34, 35 = Psalm 110:1. In Paul's sermon in Antioch (Acts 13:16-41) 9 out of 26 verses go back to the Old Testament—Acts 13:16-22 is a straight summary out of Old Testament history up to David; Acts 13:33 = Psalm 2:7; Acts 13:34 = Isaiah 55:3; Acts 13:35 = Psalm 16:10; Acts 13:41 = Habakkuk 1:5; Acts 13:47 = Isaiah 49:6. In the early days it was the Old Testament which was the sacred book of the Church.

The Order of the New Testament

Paul's Letters

How then did the New Testament arise at all? First of all, let us see in what order the New Testament was written. The most interesting fact to begin with is that the letters of Paul were almost certainly written before any of the rest of the New Testament. They were written between the years—approximately—AD 49 and AD 62.

Paul's letters were real letters. For the most part they were written to meet a local and a temporary situation. Something went wrong in Thessalonica or in Corinth and Paul wrote to correct the situation. F. C. Grant has said truly, "Had telephones been invented, Paul certainly would have used them—and we should never have had any epistles from his pen!" (F. C. Grant, *How to Read the Bible,* p. 131). Paul wrote to correct some situation in Thessalonica, or Galatia, or Corinth. He wrote as a pastor, not as an author. And it must be remembered that Paul was writing long before the days of printing. His letters *were* letters, handwritten because there was no such thing as print, existing to begin with as one single copy, often written to correct some temporary, local situation in which things had gone wrong. Of course, Paul dealt with the local and temporary situation in the light of eternal truth, but none the less his letters were letters in the real sense of the term, and there is nothing so temporary and local and evanescent as a letter. It is always of the first importance to remember that there was no question of Paul *publishing* his letters in a modern sense.

How then did they ever become Scripture? What follows is necessarily a reconstruction. It is not certainty but it does seem to meet the facts. We begin by remembering that for the most part Paul's letters existed in the churches to which they were sent and nowhere else. They were not published as books; they were sent as letters. How were they ever rescued and recovered and published? It was probably about AD 90 when the book of Acts was published. Now it is a strange thing that if we had no more than the book of Acts we would never have known that Paul ever wrote a letter. Acts has absolutely nothing to say about Paul as a letter-writer. What likely happened was that, when Acts was published, it was suddenly realized what an extraordinary figure Paul was. Suddenly Paul came to life, and in consequence of that every church which had a letter of Paul suddenly realized over again what a treasure it had; and so the letters were searched for and collected and shared and became the possession of the Church at large rather than merely the correspondence of a congregation. We may well take it that it was the publication of Acts which showed the greatness of Paul, and which was the mainspring of the movement to collect his letters. At this stage, about AD 90, Paul's letters have not yet been ranked as Scripture, but they have become one of the most treasured possessions of the Church.

The Gospels

So then Paul's letters were written between AD 49 and AD 62, and they were probably rediscovered in all their greatness as a consequence of the publication of Acts about AD 90. But what was happening to the rest of the New Testament, and in particular what was happening to the Gospels? Roughly speaking, the dates of the Gospels in the form in which we have them are AD 65–70 for Mark; AD 80–90 for Matthew and Luke; AD 100 for John. Why were they so long in being written, and why were they so long in becoming the books of the Church? And what in the end did cause them finally to be written?

The Delay in Writing Down the Gospels

In the first place, Christianity was born into a non-literary civilization, at least in its early stages. It came into the world long before the invention of printing, and there was no way of really mass-producing books as can be done in modern times. People did not think in terms of the mass-production of books as they do nowadays. This was specially true of Judaism. The Rabbis had the strongest possible objection to writing down their teaching. "Commit nothing to writing," they said. The memory of a good teacher or a good student was "like a well-plastered cistern which never loses a drop." There may well have also been a hesitation among the Jews to writing things down because, if a thing was written, it seemed in a way to challenge the authority of Scripture, and so Scripture tended to be the only thing that was written and so all other teaching was passed down by word of mouth. The *Mishnah* is what we might call the commentary on and the expansion of the laws of the Old Testament. It is the application of the written laws of the Old Testament to particular cases. It was not written down at all until the third century AD, and, when it was written down, even a summary account of it today in English translation makes a book of over 800 pages. All this was carried in the memory of the Rabbis. The written word did not have in the ancient world the place that it has today. Papias (*c.* AD 130), who was one of the great collectors of information in the early Church wrote: "I did not think that what was to be gained from books would profit me as much as what came from the living and abiding voice" (quoted, Eusebius, *The Ecclesiastical History*, 3.39.4). The first age of the Church was not a literary age in anything like the sense in which modern ages became literary, after printing was invented. At least in the East, where Christianity originated, it was much more natural to transmit knowledge and teaching by word of mouth than on the printed page.

There was further the fact that Christianity made its first impact on the poorer and the more uncultured classes. "Consider your own call, brothers," Paul writes to the Corinthians, "not many of you were wise by worldly standards, not many were powerful, not many were of noble birth" (1 Corinthians 1:26). It was indeed among the poor, and the underprivileged, and the slaves that the Christian message made its first main impact.

Early in the third century a pagan philosopher called Celsus made an attack on Christianity. He attacked it on the ground that it appealed only to the poor and the ignorant and the uncultured. He says that the attitude and the invitation of the Christians is: "Let no one cultured draw near, none wise, none sensible, for all that kind of thing we count evil; but, if any man is ignorant, if any man is wanting in sense and culture, if any man is a fool, let him come boldly... It is only the simpletons, the ignoble, the senseless, slaves and womenfolk and children whom they wish to persuade, or can persuade" (Origen, *Against Celsus,* 3.44). In its early days the Christian community was neither a book-reading nor a book-producing community.

There were, as we shall see, methods of book production which foreshadowed mass-production. But where was the market for Christian books?

Writing materials were not cheap. The writing substance which was made from the papyrus plant was produced in sheets measuring the equivalent of eight by ten inches (20.5cm by 25.5cm). One sheet cost at the cheapest the equivalent of two pence per sheet, and in the best quality range it cost five to six pence per sheet. And this has to be evaluated in the light of the fact that the average wage of a working-man was about four pence a day. In other words, it would cost about a whole day's wage to buy a single sheet of the best papyrus. Very few people are going to be able to afford books made of papyrus which cost that kind of figure.

Nor was the process of expert copying cheap, as we saw earlier. Clearly the cost would be well beyond the reach of most Christians and even of most Christian churches. The very expense of book-production tended to delay the formation of anything like a Christian literature.

So long as the original apostles continued to live, there was little demand for written books. The apostles and their immediate associates were the living books on which the Christian message was written. They were the eye-witnesses, and so long as they lived, books were not necessary.

It may well be that the factor which most of all discouraged the production of books was the belief in the imminence of the Second Coming. We have only to read a chapter like 1 Corinthians 7, where in the light of the short time before the end, as they then expected, Paul discourages marriage in a world which is hastening, as was thought, to its end. If the Second Coming was just round the corner, there was neither the time nor the reason to write books in a world in which the end was due to come at any moment.

Why the Gospels Were Written Down

These were the main factors which delayed the formation of a Christian literature; but inevitably there came a time when literature was a necessity.

The time when the story was passed down by word of mouth was bound to come to an end with the death of the apostles and of those who had been eye-witnesses. By AD 70 of the original apostles probably only John was left alive. The story had therefore to be set down. In the nature of things the written word had to take the place of "the living and abiding voice." Eusebius (*c.* 260–*c.* 339) quotes

Irenaeus' account of how the Gospels were written. Irenaeus says that after the death of Peter and Paul, "Mark, the disciple and interpreter of Peter, transmitted to us in writing those things which Peter had preached; and Luke, the attendant of Paul, recorded in a book the gospel which Paul had declared" *(Against Heresies,* 3.1.1; quoted by Eusebius, *The Ecclesiastical History,* 5.8.2, 3). The idea is that the written record was meant to take the place of the living voice. The age of the eye-witness had to come to an end; the time of the written record had come.

When Christianity went out of Palestine into the larger world, and particularly when Christianity made contact with Roman culture and civilization, it entered a society which was literate and literary, a society in which the book was part of life. Rome had its bookshops, with the pillars covered with advertisements for the latest books, and these bookshops were not only shops; they were the meeting-places of cultured society. In Rome the publishers produced books by slave labor. What happened was that fifty or a hundred slaves would write to dictation. Of course, mistakes were made, but by this mass dictation books could be copied and produced quickly and cheaply. The first book of Martial has one hundred and nineteen epigrams in about seven hundred lines of verse, and copied thus it sold for five *denarii,* which was the equivalent of about a week's wage. Once Christianity left Palestine and went out into the world of culture and literature, it went out to a world which knew all about books, and where the Christian story would soon be written down.

From the beginning Christianity was a missionary religion. It was obvious that with a world to evangelize the missionaries could not stay for any length of time in any one place. It was therefore necessary to leave a written record of the story they had told with the new converts in each place. To this day one of the first tasks of the missionary is to produce a written record of the Christian story, even if it involves the invention of an alphabet to do so. A missionary religion is almost obliged to be a literary religion.

As the Church grew and developed, there came into the Church people with strange, and even dangerous, ideas. In other words, it was not long before heresies developed. And in that situation the Church needed some "official" book, some standard account of the life and teaching of Jesus. It was precisely such that the New Testament supplied, especially in the Gospels.

We saw that one of the factors which delayed the production of a Christian literature was the supposed imminence of the Second Coming. But the Second Coming was delayed, and the Church began to see that it was living in a more or less permanent situation, and in a situation like that a written literature was no longer an irrelevance but a necessity.

In the nature of things it became necessary for the Church to produce a Christian literature.

The Accuracy of the Gospels

When we have reached this stage in our thinking about the Gospels, a question arises. We have seen that there was considerable delay in the production of a written Gospel. If Jesus was crucified round about AD 30 and if the first written Gospel did not emerge until some time between AD 65 and 70, what was happening in that thirty-five to forty years when there was no official written account of the life and teaching of Jesus? Is it possible that within this period the story of the life of Jesus and the account of his teaching grew less and less accurate, and more and more a matter of invention? From the point of view of the twentieth century that is a natural question to ask. But in the first century things were very different.

In the first place, the ancient memory was much more retentive than the modern memory. It had to be. It may well be said that the printed book, especially when the book is cheap or readily available, has tended to kill the memory. In the ancient days, people who wanted to retain some story, or some set of facts, had to do it by memorizing, because books were scarce and expensive. Xenophon tells of Niceratus. "My father," said Niceratus, "was anxious to see me develop into a good man, and as a means to this end he compelled me to memorize all Homer; and so even now I can repeat the whole *Iliad* and *Odyssey* by heart" *(Symposium, 3.6)*. The *Iliad* and the *Odyssey* each contain twenty-four books, and a book will average about five hundred lines, and this feat of memorization was something that many a Greek boy achieved as part of the education of a cultured man. Nowadays, when we want to enjoy or to refer to a passage, we look it up in a printed book; in the ancient days, when there were few or no books to look up, men carried things in their memories. There was no real fear of the story getting lost or becoming distorted in a day when the memory was strong.

But there was another process operating. There is a necessary corollary to the retentive memory. When things have to be remembered, they tend to become stereotyped. A story comes to be told always in exactly the same way. This process can be seen in the way in which children regard stories. When a child knows and loves a story, it must be told always in exactly the same way; children will not accept any deviation from the form of the story which they know and love.

So the gospel stories became stereotyped into certain *forms;* and in fairly recent years there has arisen a form of study of the Gospels called Form Criticism, which has made it its objective to find out the *forms* in which the gospel tradition circulated before it came to be set down in the shape of the written Gospels. Those who have studied these matters have identified five different kinds of forms in which the stories are stereotyped.

• There are what are called Paradigms, or Apophthegms, or Pronouncement Stories. These are pieces of tradition whose one reason for existing is that they are intended to preserve a saying of Jesus. The story is not important; the details are few; the one important thing is the saying. To take two examples—the story in Mark 2:23-28 exists simply to enshrine the saying of Jesus: "The sabbath was made for humankind, not humankind for the sabbath; so the Son of man is lord even of the sabbath." The story in Matthew 9:10-13 exists to preserve the saying of Jesus: "I have come to call not the righteous, but sinners." These stories exist, not for the sake of the story, but for the sake of the saying. The saying is the jewel of which the story is the casket.

There are stories which are called Tales or Novellen. These are stories which tell of some healing deed of Jesus. They all follow the same pattern. There is, first, a statement of the illness; second, an account of the cure; third, a statement of the consequence of the cure. To take a very simple example, there is the story of the cure of Peter's mother-in-law (Mark 1:29-31). There are:

The statement of the illness—"Now Simon's mother-in-law was in bed with a fever."

The account of the cure—"He came and took her by the hand and lifted her up. Then the fever left her."

The consequence or result—"And she began to serve them."

Nearly all of Jesus' miracles are told in this pattern. This is the stereotype which was fixed long before the story was written down.

- There are Sayings. Sayings are epigrammatic and memorable sayings of Jesus which have no context. The Pronouncement Stories with which we began all arise from an incident; the Sayings are detached sayings of Jesus. The Sermon on the Mount is almost entirely composed of such Sayings.

- We now come to two words which in this connection are used in a technical sense.

- There are Legends. In this sense and usage the word Legend does not make any kind of suggestion about whether or not the event in question actually took place. A Legend is a story, told about some holy or famous man or place, and told for religious or moral purposes. In that sense the birth and infancy stories about Jesus are Legends.

- There are Myths. Once again we must remember that this word *myth* does not express an advance verdict as to whether or not the story is true in fact. The Greeks used the word *muthos* to describe any narrative which told some story about heavenly and eternal things in terms of things of earth and time. In this sense the Temptation story and the Transfiguration story (Matthew 4:1-11; 17:2-8) are Myths because they bring on to the scene heavenly and eternal figures in circumstances of space and time.

It was in these forms that the gospel stories were quickly stereotyped in the time between the earthly life of Jesus and the writing down of the Gospels as we now have them. And there is another thing to note which is of the greatest importance. These stories were repeated over and over again for one purpose—for preaching and for the instruction of those entering the Christian community. The importance of this is that these stories were therefore never what we might call private property; they were always public possessions. If there was a change in the telling, the audience would at once ask why. They were not stories told once; they were told again and again and again. The check on them was not simply the memory of the teller, the check on them was the memory of the Christian Church. They were not simply the product of one person; they did not depend on any one person's memory. From the beginning they were the possession of the community; they were the material which preachers and teachers continually used, and to which groups of Christians continually listened. The possibility of distortion or falsification is very much reduced, when the story is being continually repeated not only to individuals but also to groups. The guarantor of the truth of any story is not any individual; the guarantor is the united witness of the Church.

The Gospels as Preaching Material

This leads us to note one more very important fact about the Gospels. The Gospels are not primarily historical documents; they are not intended to be regarded as biographies of Jesus. They are in fact the preaching material of the early Church. John tells us the aims of his Gospel: "These are written that you may come to believe that Jesus is the Christ, the Son of God, and that through believing you may have life in his name" (John 20:31). The aim is not to write a life of Jesus. Many of the things that we would look for in a biography are not there. There is, for instance, no description of what Jesus looked like. It is impossible to construct a time-table of the life of Jesus from the Gospels.

It has been said that there are two ways of writing a story. You may follow the story from day to day and from hour to hour and from event to event in strict chronological order, trying to make the record as complete as possible, and trying to leave nothing out. Or, you may take a series of significant incidents and episodes and use them as windows to see into the mind and the heart of the person you are seeking to know. It is the second method that the Gospel-writers use. They make no attempt to follow Jesus from place to place and day to day. They take a series of things he said and did to open a series of windows through which we catch glimpses of his mind and heart. It is the difference between a photograph and a portrait. A photograph shows us the subject reproduced in every detail; a portrait seizes on the special characteristics of the person being painted and brings them out. A photograph reproduces in every detail what the person looks like externally; a portrait tries to reveal his inner character and mind and heart. The Gospels are not biographies; they are not photographs; they are attempts to show the mind and the heart and the character of Jesus; and they make this attempt, not simply as a matter of interest, and not simply as a contribution to history, but so that those who read may see the mind of God in Jesus. The Gospels are not simply descriptions of Jesus; they are invitations to believe in him as the Son of God.

The Book of Acts

We have looked at the Letters of Paul and we have looked at the Gospels. There were other Letters in the New Testament also—the Letters of James and Peter and Jude and John. Between the Gospels and the Letters there comes the Book of Acts. It could be argued that Acts is the most important single book in the New Testament, for without it we would know nothing about the history of the early Church except what we could guess and deduce from the Letters. Even if we lost three of the Gospels, we would still have one left, and we would still have some kind of portrait of Jesus; but, if Acts had been lost, the history of the early Church would have been shrouded in entire darkness. It is misleading to call the book *The Acts of the Apostles.* The only apostles mentioned are James, whose death is given in one sentence (Acts 12:2), Peter, John, who is always with Peter, and who never himself speaks, and Paul. It is better to call the book Acts *of*

Apostolic Men. In the Greek title there is no *the* before either Acts or Apostles. The book does not attempt to give a comprehensive account. What it does do is to open a series of windows through which significant events in the history of the early Church may be seen.

Acts does three things. First, it tells the story of the expansion of the Church, of how, as Jesus gave his orders, the message went out from Jerusalem, to Judea and Samaria and to the ends of the earth (Acts 1:8). Second, it tells how this astonishing crusade began with no more than one hundred and twenty people (Acts 1:15), and how it was the work of the Spirit (Acts 1:8). The first great story is the story of Pentecost (Acts 2), when the Holy Spirit came. Thereafter it is the Holy Spirit who dictates every outgoing movement of the Christian Church. It was the Holy Spirit who instructed Philip to approach the Ethiopian (Acts 8:29); who told Peter to welcome the deputation from Cornelius (Acts 10:19); who was responsible for the despatch of Paul and Barnabas from Antioch on the first missionary journey (Acts 13:2); who guided the Church into receiving the Gentiles into its membership (Acts 15:28); who guided Paul's steps from Asia Minor to Europe (Acts 16:7). Acts is in reality the book of the acts of the Holy Spirit.

Third, Acts tells us of the message of the early Church. In it we have the summaries of speeches by Peter (2:14-36; 3:12-26; 4:8-12; 4:24-30); by Stephen (7:2-53); by Paul (13:16-41; 14:15-17; 17:22-31). There is no reason to doubt that, though these are not verbatim reports, they do give the substance of what early Christian sermons were about.

From them we learn the essence of the early Christian message.

- The new age has dawned, and it has dawned through the life, death and resurrection of Jesus Christ.

- Jesus' life and all that happened to him, and especially his death and resurrection, are the fulfillment of prophecy.

- He will come again to judge the living and the dead.

- Therefore repent, and receive forgiveness, and the gift of the Holy Spirit.

- Those who will not repent will reap the consequences of refusal.

One thing specially interests us about these speeches. The early Christian preachers never failed to mention the resurrection. The resurrection, as it has been put, was "the star in the firmament of early Christianity." And—very surprisingly—these early sermons do not connect the death of Jesus with the forgiveness of sins. The early Church was dominated by the resurrection faith, and by the experience of the Holy Spirit. It had not yet become what W. D. Davies has called "cross conscious." The cruciality of the cross, as P. T. Forsyth called it, and the interpretation of the cross had to wait for the great mind and heart of Paul.

The Revelation or Apocalypse

There is one book in the New Testament which is neither a Letter nor a Gospel, and it is one of the most puzzling books in the New Testament. It is the book which we call the Revelation or the Apocalypse. Although it is so strange a book to us, and although it is the only book of its kind in the New Testament, it is in fact a specimen of a kind of book which was very common in the days when the New Testament books were being written.

The Jews divided all time into two ages. There was this present age, and, as they saw it, this present age is wholly bad; it is so bad that it cannot be reformed; it is fit only to be destroyed. Contrasted with this there is the age which is to come, and as they believed, the age which is to come is the golden age of God, when everything will be as God meant it to be, and when the good will enter into their joy and the evil into their destruction. The question is, how was the one age to turn into the other? How was the evil of this present age to become the glory of the age which is to come? By the time of the New Testament the Jews were sure that this change could never come about by human means; it could not come about by any process of reformation. It could come about only by the total destruction of this present age, and the birth of a new age which would be the age of God. How then would the change take place? They believed that it would take place at the Day of the Lord. The Day of the Lord would be a time when the present world and all that is in it would disintegrate and be destroyed, when there would be a last and final judgment, and when there would arise out of the chaos a new world which would be the world of God recreated for the people of God.

So there came into being a whole series of books, each of them called an Apocalypse. The word "Apocalypse" literally means an unveiling. And the aim of these books was to tell of the terrible events of the last days, of the terror of judgment and of the golden age which was to come. In the nature of things these books were unintelligible except to those who understood the "code," for the books were seeking to tell of things which no eye had seen, which no ear had heard, and which had never entered into the minds of men. Many of these books survive, for the darker the history of the Jewish people, the harder their fate, the sorer their subjugation and slavery, the more eagerly they dreamed of the day when God would invade history, when the dramatic change would come, and when the new age would dawn. Mostly these are Jewish books, but our Apocalypse is a Christian specimen of this kind of literature, and this is why it is the most difficult book in the New Testament for us to understand. But it must be remembered that, strange as it is, it is a specimen of one of the commonest kinds of religious literature in New Testament times.

The Final Formation of the New Testament

So, then, as we have it now, the New Testament is composed of the four Gospels, Acts, a series of Letters written by Paul, James, Peter, John, Jude and others, and one Apocalypse. Most people would agree that it took somewhere around seventy years to write. The Letter to the Galatians is probably the earliest book in it—about AD 49—and the Second Letter of Peter is probably the latest book in it—about AD 120; and having been written, as we have already seen, the New Testament took until AD 367 to assume the form in which we have it today.

There are certain milestones on the way to the completion of the New Testament at which we must now look. The great steps in the final definition of the contents of the New Testament were the result of the mistakes into which certain heretics tried to lead the Church.

Marcion

The first of these heretics was Marcion. He was a wealthy ship-owner from Sinope on the Black Sea coast and he came to Rome about AD 140. Marcion was a Gnostic. The Gnostics—from a word meaning "knowledge"—were among the most dangerous heretics who ever threatened the Church. They set out to explain the existence of sin and evil. Their basic assumption was that from the beginning of time there have been two principles—matter and spirit, matter and God. Matter was not created; it, as the Gnostics believed, was a basic substance which was always there. It is the basic material out of which the world was made. This matter was essentially evil, just as spirit is essentially good. This is to say that from the beginning the world is made out of flawed material. That is the explanation of sorrow and sin and suffering and pain. The world is made out of bad stuff. But, if matter is evil, this means that the true God who is spirit and who is altogether good could not have touched it. And this means that the true and good God, who is spirit, cannot have been responsible for creation. What happened, as the Gnostics taught, was that the good God put out a series of emanations or aeons, each one more distant from himself. Each emanation was more ignorant of God, and at the end of the scale there was an emanation who was not only ignorant of God, but also hostile to God; and it was this distant, ignorant, hostile emanation who was the creator of the world. This meant that the Gnostics believed that all created things, including the body, are essentially evil. All matter is bad and only spirit is good.

And then the Gnostics took another step. They held that the creator, the distant, hostile, ignorant emanation is the God of the Old Testament, and the real God, the God of spirit, the true God, is the God of the New Testament. This had one obvious consequence. The Gnostic completely, totally and altogether abandoned and discarded the Old Testament. The Old Testament was the book of the ignorant and hostile God. But it also meant that everything in the New Testament which had anything to do with the God of the Old Testament had to go. So of the Christian books Marcion kept only an expurgated version of Luke's Gospel. But Paul was Marcion's hero, for Marcion misunderstood Paul and thought that Paul's attack on the Law was an attack on the Old Testament, and so Marcion kept the Letters of Paul as his most sacred books. So just as the Old Testament consisted of the Law and the Prophets, Marcion's Christian book consisted of the Gospel—Luke—and the Apostle—Paul. Clearly, this was something to which the Church had to offer an answer.

Marcion's attack left the Church with two obligations. First, the Church had to define its attitude to the Old Testament, which Marcion wished completely to discard, and it had also to make up its mind just what books composed the New Testament. The Church affirmed its faith in the Old Testament; it had no intention of jettisoning it. And there are signs that the Church did face up to the task of defining the New Testament.

There exists a list of New Testament books formulated about AD 170. It is called the Muratorian Canon, after the discoverer of it. It is slightly mutilated at the beginning, but it is easy to see just what it contained. Its contents were as follows—the four Gospels, Matthew, Mark, Luke, John; the Acts of the Apostles; Paul's Letters, which it enumerates in the unusual order Corinthians, Ephesians, Philippians, Colossians, Galatians, Thessalonians, Romans; to these it adds the Pastoral Epistles, that is, the Letters to Timothy and to Titus, and the Letter to Philemon; it includes the Letter of Jude and the First and Second Letters of John; and the Revelation. It included the Wisdom of Solomon, and—with a doubt—a second Apocalypse, the Apocalypse of Peter. The one surprise is the omission of First Peter. The other books which are omitted—James, Second Peter, Third John, Hebrews—are the books which took longest to make their place in the canon of the New Testament unquestioned and secure. So we can see that towards the end of the second century the New Testament is well on the way to being in the form which it finally took.

Montanus

For the moment we must turn aside from the story of the final formation of the New Testament to another question. How did the process of writing the New Testament come to an end? Why and when did the Christian Church come to the conclusion that no more New Testament books could be written, or, to put it more accurately, when did the Church decide, and why, that the quota of sacred books was complete and not to be added to any more?

This too happened under the influence of a heretic. Some time towards the end of the second century a man called Montanus appeared on the scene. Montanus felt that the original standards of the Church had been lowered. He remembered that Jesus had said that the Spirit would come to the Church, and bring the Church fresh truth and fresh strength. As the Fourth Gospel put it, Jesus had said: "I still have many things to say to you, but you cannot bear them now. When the Spirit of truth comes, he will guide you into all the truth ... He will take what is mine and declare it to you" (John 16:12-14). Jesus had promised that the Holy Spirit, the Paraclete, would come, and would, as it were, develop and complete his message. What happened was that Montanus arrived on the scene and claimed that he in fact was the promised Paraclete and that he proposed to give the new revelation which Jesus had promised.

This indeed presented the Church with a problem; and the Church solved it by holding that the revelation of God had been given and completed, and that the days of revelation in the full sense of the term were ended. The Church in effect declared that all the sacred books which should be written had been written, and that Scripture was closed. As Tertullian, who later became a Montanist, put it bitterly, the Holy Spirit had been chased into a book. In any event, the canon of Scripture was regarded as closed. It would never have done, so the Church felt, if every now and then someone were to come up with an entirely new revelation. There had to be a time of full revelation by which all other revelations were to be judged. It was decided that that time had come and that no more sacred books could be written. It was not that they had ceased to believe in the revealing power of the Holy Spirit. The difference was that in the first days the Holy Spirit had enabled men to write the sacred books of the Christian religion; in the later days the Holy Spirit enabled men to understand, to interpret and to apply what had been written.

Apostolic Authorship

What then was the qualification for a book to gain entry into the Church's list of supremely sacred books? The one question asked was whether or not a book was apostolic—that is, whether or not it was written by an actual apostle, or at least by an apostolic man. Thus, as far as the Gospels go, Matthew and John were the work of apostles, and Mark and Luke qualified, because Mark was held to be the disciple and the interpreter of Peter, while Luke was held to have put down in a book the gospel preached by Paul (Irenaeus, *Against Heresies,* 3.1.1, 2; Eusebius, *The Ecclesiastical History,* 5.8.2). This was in the end why the Letter to the Hebrews was ascribed to Paul. It was known well enough that it was not actually the writing of Paul. As Origen said in the famous sentence: "Who wrote the Letter to the Hebrews only God really knows" (Eusebius, 6.25.11–14). Paul was the great letter writer; the Letter to the Hebrews was so valuable that the Church wanted to keep it as one of the sacred books; and so to give it the status it needed it was added to the Letters of Paul.

There was a good reason for making apostolic authorship the standard of acceptance of any book as one of the Church's sacred and authoritative books. Christianity is an historical religion. Christianity took its origin and its power from an historical person, Jesus of Nazareth. Therefore the one necessity was an unbroken chain of evidence going right back to him. The world was full of the stories of dying and rising gods. The only way to make it certain that the Christian gospel was not simply another of these stories was to trace it back to some one who could say: "I know that this is true, because with my own eyes I saw it."

This stressing of apostolic authorship had one interesting consequence. On general grounds it seems strange that the Church kept four different Gospels. The fact that there were four Gospels could produce embarrassing situations. For instance, the Fourth Gospel has the incident of the cleansing of the Temple at the beginning of the ministry of Jesus, and the other three have it at the end. The fact that there are four Gospels often produces problems of harmonization. There was an experiment in harmonizing the Gospels made by a man called Tatian about AD 180. Tatian produced the *Diatessaron,* which literally means "through four," and in it he made a harmony of the Gospels in which by a scissors and paste method he managed to include almost everything. A fragment of the *Diatessaron* reads like this:

> *And the day was Preparation; the Sabbath was dawning (Luke 23:54). And when it was evening, on the Preparation, that is the day before the Sabbath (Matthew 27:57; Mark 15:42), there came up a man, being a member of the council (Matthew 27:57; Luke 23:50), from Arimathaea, a city of Judah, by name Joseph (Matthew 27:57; Luke 23:50), good and righteous, being a disciple of Jesus, but secretly for fear of the Jews (Matthew 27:57; Luke 23:50; John 19:38). And he was looking for the kingdom of God (Luke 23:51). This man had not consented to their purpose (Luke 23:51).*

It is true that Tatian's *Diatessaron* was not put together with any great artistry, but one would have expected the four Gospels to be woven into one narrative. What stopped that was the overwhelming importance of apostolic testimony. The Gospels were all of them the work of apostolic men or of apostles; and it was therefore more important to keep them as they were than to harmonize them. So much so, that on their being four Gospels, Irenaeus could write: "As there are four quarters of the world in which we live, as there are four universal winds, and as the Church is scattered all over the earth, and the gospel is the pillar and base of the Church and the breath of life, it is likely that it should have four pillars breathing immortality on every side and kindling afresh the life of men. Whence it is evident that the Word, the architect of all things, who sits upon the cherubim and holds all things together, having been made manifest to men, gave us the gospel in a fourfold shape, but held together by one Spirit" *(Against Heresies,* 3.11.8). So in the end it came to be argued that it was just as natural that there should be four Gospels as that there should be four points of the compass.

So then the Gospels and the Letters took their place as the books of the Church; and that place became secure when they began to be read at the public worship of the Church. When, as the years passed on, they became part of every service of the Church, they were fully established.

Origen and Eusebius

We may complete this story by noting still one other thing. For a time there were certain books whose position was not secure. Two of the great early scholars of the Church made investigations about the contents of the Christian Scriptures.

The first was Origen who lived from AD 185 to 254. In his time the situation was that the place of the four Gospels, of the Letters of Paul, including Hebrews, of 1 Peter, 1 John and the Revelation was undisputed and secure. Origen goes on to say that Peter may have left another Letter, but that this was doubtful. Second and Third John he knew but not everyone, he said, considered them genuine. And James and Jude he never mentions at all.

The second was Eusebius of Caesarea, the great church historian. He divided the books of the Church into three classes—the universally accepted, the disputed and the spurious. The universally accepted are the four Gospels, Acts, the Letters of Paul, including Hebrews, 1 John and 1 Peter. The Revelation hovered between the universally accepted and the disputed. The disputed books are James, Jude, 2 Peter and 2 and 3 John. He says that 2 Peter is not generally accepted, but that because it has been found profitable by many it may well be Scripture. He says that many regard the Letter of James as spurious, and that very few of the early writers of the Church have ever mentioned it. The list of Eusebius is to all intents and purposes the same as that of Origen.

Athanasius

So finally we come to the last stage. The first time, as we began by saying, that we find the books of the New Testament listed exactly as we have them today is in the Easter Letter of Athanasius to his people in the year AD 367, and it marks such an epoch that the relevant section must be quoted in full:

> *There must be no hesitation to state again the books of the New Testament, for they are these: Four Gospels, according to Matthew, according to Mark, according to Luke and according to John. Further, after these, also the Acts of the Apostles, and the seven so-called Catholic Epistles of the Apostles, as follows: one of James, but two of Peter, then three of John, and after these one of Jude; in addition to these there are fourteen Epistles of the apostle Paul put down in the following order: the first to the Romans, then two to the Corinthians, and after these the Epistles to the Galatians, and then to the Ephesians: further, the Epistles to the Philippians and to the Colossians and two to the Thessalonians, and the Epistle to the Hebrews. And next two Letters to Timothy, but one to Titus, and the last one to Philemon. Moreover also, the Apocalypse of John.*

Here for the first time is the complete New Testament as we know it.

Luther

So then by AD 367 the New Testament was completed and the canon was closed. There was never again to be any variation in it. It is, however, worth while to see what Luther has to say on the subject. To us nowadays the attitude of the Reformers seems quite astonishingly free and radical. They claimed a sovereign liberty in regard to the place they gave to certain books. Luther had only one touchstone, and he expressed it with his usual vivid violence: "That which does not teach Christ is not apostolic, though Peter or Paul should have said it; on the contrary, that which does preach Christ is apostolic, even if it should come from Judas, Annas, Herod, or Pilate."

There were certain books to which Luther gave a supreme place, and certain books to which he gave a secondary place. There are twenty-seven books in the New Testament. On the title page of his own translation of the New Testament Luther printed and numbered twenty-three of them; then at the end in a little group of their own, indented and not numbered, he placed James, Hebrews, Jude and the

Revelation. James, he said, was "an epistle of straw; for it has nothing of the nature of the gospel about it." It teaches justification by works; it contradicts Paul; and it has nothing to say about the life and the death and the resurrection of Jesus, and about the Holy Spirit. Hebrews in three places in Chapters 6, 10, 12, says that there can be no repentance after baptism, and this, says Luther, is in flat contradiction to the teaching of the Gospels and of Paul. Jude is no more than an extract from 2 Peter; it is in fact included very largely in 2 Peter. As for the Revelation, Luther said of it: "I hold it to be neither apostolic nor prophetic. . . . My spirit cannot acquiesce in the book." He went on to say: "I abide by the books which present Christ pure and clear... After all, in it Christ is neither taught nor acknowledged."

Luther's standards were completely clear. In his Preface to the New Testament he writes—and we must quote the passage in full:

John's Gospel and St. Paul's epistles, especially that to the Romans, and St. Peter's first Epistle are the true kernel and marrow of all the books...

In them you find not many works and miracles of Christ described, but you do find it depicted, in masterly fashion, how faith in Christ overcomes sin, death and hell, and gives life, righteousness and salvation. This is the real nature of the Gospel... If I had to do without one or the other—either the works or the preaching of Christ—I would rather do without his works than his preaching; for the works do not help me, but his words give life, as he himself says... Now John writes very little about the works of Christ, but very much about his preaching; therefore John's Gospel is the one, tender, true, chief Gospel, far, far to be preferred to the other three and placed high above them. So too the Epistles of St. Paul and St. Peter far surpass the other three Gospels—Matthew, Mark and Luke.

In a word, John's Gospel and his First Epistle, St. Paul's Epistles, especially Romans, Galatians and Ephesians, and St. Peter's First Epistle are the books that show you Christ and teach you all that is necessary and good for you to know, even though you were never to see or hear any other book or doctrine.

Luther has no hesitation in drawing distinctions between the books of the New Testament. He makes it clear that this preference is a personal thing. At the end of his Introduction to James he writes: "Therefore, I cannot put him among the chief books, though I would not thereby prevent anyone from putting him where he pleases and estimating him as he pleases, for there are many good things in him."

For Luther all the New Testament books were holy, but within the New Testament there was a special Holy of Holies of books where above all Jesus Christ is to be encountered.

This then is the story of how the New Testament came to be what it is today, and although to Luther and others there have always been some books which are dearer and more precious than others, for the last sixteen hundred years no book has been added and no book has been taken away.

3.

The Apocrypha

WE HAVE NOW studied the story of the making of the Old Testament and the making of the New Testament. But there is still another group of books at which we must look. These books form what is known as the Apocrypha. These books are often bound in with the Old and the New Testament in one composite volume. We cannot say that they are universally regarded as part of the Bible as the Old and New Testaments are. But we certainly cannot pass them over in silence, because for the Roman Catholic Church these books are an integral part of the Bible and for the Anglican Church they have a considerable share in the Church's lectionary, and they are regarded as at least sacred and profitable books.

The Meaning of "Apocrypha"

We must begin by looking at the meaning of the word *Apocrypha*. The word is a Greek neuter plural from the word *apokruphon,* and it means things which ought to be kept secret and hidden away. This word is applied to three different kinds of books or information.

- It was applied to books which were too difficult, too sacred, or too holy for common use. As we have seen, 2 Esdras (4 Ezra) 14:19-48 has the story of how Ezra restored the sacred books when they had been burned and destroyed in the days of the exile. The story is legendary, but it does show the place that Ezra had in popular thought and it does illustrate the kind of thing meant by this first use of the word *apokrupha*.

It was Ezra's task to rewrite the lost law. He was told to take five scribes who were trained to write rapidly. They proceeded to an open field. There Ezra was given a cup. "It was full of something like water, but its color was like fire." Ezra drank it and began to dictate. The dictation went on for forty days, during which ninety-four books were dictated and written. Then the Most High said to Ezra: "Make public the twenty-four books that you wrote first and let the worthy and the unworthy read them; but keep the seventy that were written last, in order to give them to the wise among your people. For in them is the spring of understanding, the fountain of wisdom, and the river of knowledge." The twenty-four books were the books of the Old Testament. What the others were we cannot tell, but the point is that the idea of books to be kept secret from the ordinary person was a familiar enough idea. So then the first meaning of the word *apocrypha* is *secret*, because too sacred and too lofty for ordinary use.

- There is a modern use of the word *apocryphal* which is the very opposite of that. If nowadays we describe a story as apocryphal, we mean that it is fictitious. An apocryphal story is the opposite of a true story. The word is used to describe the legendary tales which often gather round distinguished people. In this sense the word apocryphal describes something inferior rather than something superior.

- But when the word *apocrypha* is used to describe these books of which we are at present thinking, the main meaning of it is that the books in question are not to be read in public and at public worship, but there is no objection to their being read privately at home for instruction and profit. This is the prevailing Protestant use of the word. The Roman Catholic Church does not call these books The Apocrypha at all. For it they are fully and truly Scripture. But, generally speaking, for the Protestant Church the term denotes a book of secondary significance, admittedly useful, but not to be ranked with books which are unquestionably Scripture.

The Books of the Apocrypha

First, then, what are the books which are included among the Apocrypha? These books number fourteen or fifteen:

- 1 Esdras
- 2 Esdras (sometimes referred to as 4 Ezra)
- Tobit
- Judith
- The Additions to the Book of Esther
- The Wisdom of Solomon
- Ecclesiasticus, or the Wisdom of Jesus the Son of Sirach
- Baruch
- The Letter of Jeremiah
- The Prayer of Azariah and the Song of the Three Young Men
- Susanna
- Bel and the Dragon
- The Prayer of Manasseh
- The First Book of the Maccabees
- The Second Book of the Maccabees

That list comprises fifteen books; but sometimes the Letter of Jeremiah is included as the last chapter of Baruch, and then the number becomes fourteen.

These fifteen books fall into various types and classifications.

Additions to Old Testament books

There are books which are additions to books which are already in the Old Testament.

There are the Additions to Esther. In the Book of Esther as it stands in the Old Testament, there is not one single mention of the name of God, and there is not one single instance of anyone at prayer. All the additions except one mention the name of God, and one mentions the name of God no fewer than nine times in nine verses, while in another of the additions both Esther and Mordecai are shown at prayer. These additions are designed to supply what was wanting in the original book.

The Prayer of Azariah and the Song of the Three Young Men, Susanna and Bel and the Dragon are all additions to Daniel. Azariah is the Hebrew name of Abed-nego, and the Prayer and the Song are put into the mouths of the three young men in the burning fiery furnace. The Prayer is one of the great praising prayers of the world. Here are some verses from it:

> *Bless the Lord, sun and moon;*
> *sing praise to him*
> *and highly exalt him forever.*
> *Bless the Lord, stars of heaven;*
> *sing praise to him*
> *and highly exalt him forever.*
> *Bless the Lord, all rain and dew;*
> *sing praise to him*
> *and highly exalt him forever.*
> *Bless the Lord, all you winds;*
> *sing praise to him*
> *and highly exalt him forever.*
> *Bless the Lord, fire and heat;*
> *sing praise to him*
> *and highly exalt him forever.*
> *Bless the Lord, winter cold and summer heat;*
> *sing praise to him*
> *and highly exalt him forever.*
> *Bless the Lord, dews and falling snow;*
> *sing praise to him*
> *and highly exalt him forever.*
> *Bless the Lord, nights and days;*
> *sing praise to him*

> *and highly exalt him forever.*
> *Bless the Lord, light and darkness;*
>   *sing praise to him*
>   *and highly exalt him forever.*
> *Bless the Lord, ice and cold;*
>   *sing praise to him*
>   *and highly exalt him forever.*
> *Bless the Lord, frosts and snows;*
>   *sing praise to him*
>   *and highly exalt him forever.*
> *Bless the Lord, lightnings and clouds;*
>   *sing praise to him*
>   *and highly exalt him forever.*
> *Let the earth bless the Lord;*
>   *let it sing praise to him*
>   *and highly exalt him forever. (verses 40-52)*

The other two additional pieces to Daniel have a fame all their own, for they are designed to show the wisdom of Daniel, and they are perhaps the two earliest detective stories in the literature of the world. Dorothy Sayers included them at the beginning of her *Omnibus of Crime* published in 1929.

Susanna is the story of a beautiful and virtuous woman. Two Jewish elders conceived a guilty passion for her. On one summer day Susanna informed her maids that she wished to bathe in the pool in her garden. The two elders concealed themselves in the garden and, while Susanna was bathing sprang out, and sought to seduce her. She refused their requests; they said that, if she did not yield to them, they would say that they had discovered her in the garden in the arms of a lover. She refused them. They made their charges, and, since they were known and respected elders, Susanna was found guilty. Daniel appeared and asked for a retrial, which was granted. Daniel examined each of the elders separately. He asked each of them the same question. "Under what kind of tree did you see Susanna in the embrace of her lover?" "A mastic tree," the first said. "An evergreen oak," the second said. It was seen at once that their story was fictitious, and Susanna was vindicated. So the story is an exercise in cross-examination.

There are two stories in Bel and the Dragon. Bel was the great god of the Babylonians. Daniel insisted to the king that Bel was nothing but a lifeless idol. "How then," demanded the king, "does he consume the vast amount of food that is left in the temple for him each night?" For every night there were left in the temple twelve bushels of fine flour, forty sheep and fifty gallons of wine. Daniel knew that the priests had an underground entrance into the temple. So the offerings were put into the temple, and the doors were locked, and the building was left for the night. But unknown to anyone Daniel had covered the floor of the temple with fine powdered ash. Sure enough, in the morning all the food was gone; and the priests clamored for Daniel's death. But Daniel told the king to look at the floor of the temple, and there in the ash were the crowded footprints of men, women and children, and the deception of the priests was exposed, and Bel for ever discredited.

No doubt these stories were never meant to be taken as history. They are what one writer has called "moralistic novels," but to this day they remain among the great short stories of the world's literature.

Stories

There are two magnificent stories on the list. There is Tobit, the charming story of the journey of Tobias in the company of Raphael the angel, who disguised himself as a man, and with the little dog. And there is the bloodthirsty thriller of Judith, who in the days of her country's peril, made her way into the hostile camp, deceived Holofernes the Assyrian general into thinking that he might have his way with her, made him blind drunk, cut off his head, and brought it home in a bag—one of the great scenarios of the world!

Maybe Shakespeare knew and loved these stories, for he called his daughters Susanna and Judith!

Didactic Books

There are two long didactic books. They belong to what is called the Wisdom Literature. The word Wisdom used of that kind of literature does not refer to philosophic and intellectual wisdom; it refers to the practical wisdom which enables a man to live a good life both in the eyes of men and the sight of God. The Wisdom of Solomon was written sometime late in the first century BC or in the first century AD. It is a long book with some magnificent passages in it. We choose one which brings comfort to those in trouble or who face death:

> *The souls of the righteous are in the hand of God,*
> *and no torment will ever touch them.*
> *In the eyes of the foolish they seemed to have died,*
> *and their departure was thought to be disaster,*
> *and their going from us to be their destruction;*
> *but they are at peace.*
> *For though in the sight of others they were punished,*
> *their hope is full of immortality.*
> *Having been disciplined a little, they will receive great good,*
> *because God tested them and found them worthy of himself.*
> *(Wisdom of Solomon 3:1-5)*

The book was attributed to Solomon, because Solomon was the man whose name above all was connected with true wisdom.

The other of the great Wisdom books of the Apocrypha is entitled "The Wisdom of Jesus the son of Sirach," or, to call it by its better known name, Ecclesiasticus. It was originally written in Hebrew about 180 BC, and about fifty years later the grandson of the original writer took it to Egypt and translated it into Greek.

There are many famous passages in Ecclesiasticus, of which perhaps the most famous of all is the long section in praise of famous men (Chapters 44–50). Especially famous is the introduction to that section (44:1-15):

> *Let us now sing the praises of famous men,*
> *our ancestors in their generations.*
> *The Lord apportioned to them great glory,*
> *his majesty from the beginning.*
> *There were those who ruled in their kingdoms,*
> *and made a name for themselves by their valour;*

those who gave counsel because they were intelligent;
those who spoke in prophetic oracles;
those who led the people by their counsels
and by their knowledge of the people's lore;
they were wise in their words of instruction;
those who composed musical tunes,
and put verses in writing…
All these were honoured in their generations,
and were the pride of their times.
Some of them have left behind a name,
so that others declare their praise.
But of others there is no memory;
they have perished as though they had never existed…
Their bodies are buried in peace,
but their name lives on generation after generation.
The assembly declares their wisdom,
and the congregation proclaims their praise.

It is in Ecclesiasticus that there is the famous tribute to doctors (38:1-14):

Honour physicians for their services,
for the Lord created them;
for their gift of healing comes from the Most High,
and they are rewarded by the king.
The skill of physicians makes them distinguished,
and in the presence of the great they are admired.
The Lord created medicines out of the earth,
and the sensible will not despise them…
By them he heals and takes away pain;
the pharmacist makes a mixture from them.
His works will never be finished;
and from him health spreads over all the earth…
There may come a time when recovery lies in the hands of physicians,
for they too pray to the Lord
that he grant them success in diagnosis
and in healing, for the sake of preserving life.

There is still another famous passage in which Sirach holds that only the man of leisure can ever become a great scholar and teacher, and that wisdom is not possible for the workers of the world. But, having said that, he pays the workers a great tribute (38:31-34):

> *All these rely on their hands,*
> *and all are skilful in their own work.*
> *Without them no city can be inhabited,*
> *and wherever they live, they will not go hungry.*
> *Yet they are not sought out for the council of the people,*
> *nor do they attain eminence in the public assembly.*
> *They do not sit in the judge's seat,*
> *nor do they understand the decisions of the courts;*
> *they cannot expound discipline or judgment,*
> *and they are not found among the rulers.*
> *But they maintain the fabric of the world,*
> *and their concern is for the exercise of their trade.*

The Wisdom of Solomon and Ecclesiasticus are two very great books. From its earliest days the Church knew and valued them, and urged its members to read them. There are not a few who would gladly see them in the canon of Scripture.

Historical books

There are certain books in the Apocrypha which have to do with historical events. There is 1 Esdras, which does no more than retrace the ground covered in part of 2 Chronicles and in Ezra and Nehemiah. It has only one additional passage in it, and that the origin of a famous proverbial saying. As the Authorized Version of the Bible has it: "Great is the Truth and mighty above all things."

The other two historical books are 1 and 2 Maccabees. These are important because in their different ways they tell the story of the famous fight for freedom in which Judas Maccabaeus is the most famous name. Of 1 Maccabees Martin Luther said that it was "not unworthy to be reckoned among the books of Scripture."

Devotional books

There is one book which we might call devotional. This is The Prayer of Manasseh. Manasseh, as the Hebrew historian saw him, was one of the worst of the kings (2 Kings 21:1-18; 2 Chronicles 33:1-20). He reigned for fifty-five years; he was guilty of "the abominable practices" of the heathen nations of the land. He built altars to Baal; he worshipped "the host of heaven"; he offered his son as a sacrifice; he kept mediums and magicians. He set up a graven image of Asherah in the very temple itself, and he shed innocent blood. For this the Babylonions were to be unloosed against Judaea, the temple was to be destroyed and the people were to be banished (2 Kings 24:3). The Chronicler tells us that for a time Manasseh himself was in exile. They "took Manasseh with hooks and bound him with fetters of bronze and brought him to Babylon." There in captivity Manasseh repented of all his evil ways and prayed to God, and God brought him back to Jerusalem. God heard his prayer and received his entreaty (2 Chronicles 33:10-19). The Prayer of Manasseh is supposed to be the prayer that Manasseh prayed in the bitterness of his exile, and the aim of his single-page work is to show that, even for a Manasseh, there is forgiveness, if he repents before God. Here are some verses from it:

> *I have sinned, O Lord, I have sinned,*
> *   and I acknowledge my transgressions.*
> *I earnestly implore you,*
> *   forgive me, O Lord, forgive me!*
> *   Do not destroy me with my transgressions!*
> *Do not be angry with me forever or store up evil for me;*
> *   do not condemn me to the depths of the earth.*
> *For you, O Lord, are the God of those who repent,*
> *   and in me you will manifest your goodness;*
> *for, unworthy as I am, you will save me according to your great mercy,*
> *   and I will praise you continually all the days of my life.*
> *For all the host of heaven sings your praise,*
> *   and yours is the glory forever.*
> *Amen. (verses 12-15)*

Here is the confidence that, if he repents, the worst of sinners can be saved.

Prophetic books

There are two books which are in the prophetic succession. The first is the book of Baruch, written probably in the first century BC, and purporting to be written by Baruch the secretary of Jeremiah (Jeremiah 36:4). Sometimes the Letter of Jeremiah is appended to Baruch as a sixth chapter. The Letter of Jeremiah is a scathing indictment of idolatry. It must come from a time when the Jews were tempted and invited to share the idolatrous worship of their neighbors. It is the craftsmen who make the idols. "People take gold and make crowns for the heads of their gods, as they would for a girl who loves ornaments." And sometimes the priests steal the gold, and gold can be spent even in a brothel. The dust of the temple gathers on them and they have to be cleaned and dusted down. Bats, swallows, birds and cats sit on them. If they have to be moved they have to be carried, because they have no feet of their own. If you put them down, they tip over and collapse and have to be hoisted up again. "They cannot save a man from death or rescue the weak from the strong. They cannot restore sight to a blind man; they cannot rescue a man who is in distress." The men who manufacture them are dying men—how can they make gods? If the temple goes on fire, the priests can flee and rescue themselves, but the gods can only burn helplessly. They are no better than a scarecrow in a garden.

In this little pamphlet idolatry is blasted with ridicule, which even yet is effective.

Apocalyptic Literature

Lastly, there is one apocalyptic book. This is 2 Esdras, or, as it is sometimes called, 4 Ezra. We have already seen that apocalyptic literature deals with the terrible end-time when this present age and all its evil will be destroyed, and when the Day of the Lord will come, and the new age of God's Kingdom will be born. That time is to be a time of complete destruction and of utter disintegration. These apocalyptic books, as we have seen, describe the indescribable, and tell of the things which no eye has seen, no ear has heard and no mind has conceived. They are unintelligible except to the initiated, and 4 Ezra is no exception. Luther found it so bizarre that, when he translated the Apocrypha, he did not even attempt to translate this book. In his characteristically violent way he said that he threw it into the Elbe!

Second Esdras took a long time in the writing. The basis of it is Chapters 3 to 14, which purports to be the record of seven revelations given to Ezra in Babylon. This part was written about AD 100. This section was originally written in Aramaic. It was later translated into Greek. The Aramaic version of it is lost, and so is the Greek, except for two or three verses. The version in which it exists is the Latin version. About AD 150 an anonymous and unknown Christian writer added Chapters 1 and 2 in Greek. And about AD 250 still another unknown Christian writer added Chapters 15 and 16. It had always been clear that there was some kind of gap between 7:35 and 7:36. In 1874 the missing Latin text of these verses turned up and were inserted into the text.

A brief illustration of the visions of this strange book is taken from Chapter 5:

> *The sun shall suddenly begin to shine at night,*
> *and the moon during the day.*
> *Blood shall drip from wood,*
> *and the stone shall utter its voice;*
> *the peoples shall be troubled,*
> *and the stars shall fall. (5:4-5)*

This is a book which has little or nothing to say to us nowadays.

Sources of the Apocrypha

We have now seen what the Apocrypha are, and we must go on to ask where the books came from, and why their position is doubtful. The answer to the first part of this question is that the books of the Apocrypha appear in the Greek version of the Old Testament, but not in the original Hebrew. The Greek version of the Old Testament is called the Septuagint. In the reign of Ptolemy the Second Philadelphus, which extended from 285 to 246 BC, the Old Testament was translated into Greek in Egypt. This was the fitting place for that translation to be made, because at that time there were more than a million Jews in Egypt, many of whom had never been in Palestine. These Jews had either forgotten, or had never known, Hebrew. Greek was the language they used. The Septuagint—it is usually designated by the letters LXX, the Latin form of the number 70, which was the number of its translators—is one of the most important books in the world, because it was that which made the Old Testament available to nearly everyone, for everyone knew Greek and only a few people knew Hebrew. In due time the Septuagint was to be the basis of the first translation of the Old Testament into Latin, and therefore the earliest Latin Old Testament had the same form as the Greek Old Testament. We will see what happened if we set down side by side, in the order in which they occur, the books of the Old Testament in its Hebrew, Greek, Latin and English versions (see table opposite).

It can be seen at once that the Hebrew, the Greek, the Latin and the English Bible differ widely in the books which they do and do not contain, and just as widely in the order in which they have the books.

From the lists one thing is clear—the Greek Old Testament, the Septuagint, is by far the most inclusive. It includes even books which are not in the official Apocrypha, for example 3 and 4 Maccabees, the Odes, and the Psalms of Solomon. Why should this be? As we have seen, for the Jews of Palestine the sacred writings comprised twenty-four books and no more; their canon was closed. "If anyone," said the Rabbis, "receives more than twenty-four books, he introduces confusion into his house." By the Jewish law it was illegal to carry a burden on the Sabbath day, and it was laid down that, if there was a fire in a house, only the twenty-four books could be carried out and no more. On the other hand, the Jews of Alexandria had much wider sympathies. For them, if a book was inspiring, it was inspired. So in the early days there were the two versions of the Old Testament, the limited version of the Palestinian Jews and the inclusive version of the Greek-speaking Jews; and the extra books in the Greek version are the

Apocrypha. And since in the early days far more people used the Greek than the Hebrew Old Testament, there was a time when these extra books were very widely received.

Have we then reached a stage at which there were two Old Testaments—a shorter Hebrew one and a larger Greek one? The Apocrypha form quite a considerable unit of material. Bruce Metzger expresses it statistically:

	Books	*Chapters*	*Verses*
Old Testament	39	929	23,214
New Testament	27	260	7,959
Apocrypha	14/15	183	6,081

Hebrew	**Greek Septuagint**	**Latin**	**English**
The Law	*The Law*	*Historical Books*	Genesis
Genesis	Genesis	Genesis	Exodus
Exodus	Exodus	Exodus	Leviticus
Leviticus	Leviticus	Leviticus	Numbers
Numbers	Numbers	Numbers	Deuteronomy
Deuteronomy	Deuteronomy	Deuteronomy	Joshua
		Joshua	Judges
The Prophets	*The Histories*	Judges	Ruth
Joshua	Joshua	Ruth	1 and 2
Judges	Judges	1 and 2 Kings	Samuel
1 and 2 Samuel	Ruth	3 and 4 Kings	1 and 2 Kings
1 and 2 Kings	1 and 2 Kings	1 and 2	1 and 2
Isaiah	(= 1 and 2	Chronicles	Chronicles
Jeremiah	Samuel)	1 Esdras	Ezra
Ezekiel	3 and 4 Kings	(= Ezra)	Nehemiah
Hosea	(= 1 and 2)	2 Esdras	Esther
Joel	Kings)	(= Nehemiah)	Job
Amos	1 and 2	Tobit	Psalms
Obadiah	Chronicles	Judith	Proverbs
Jonah	1 Esdras	Esther	Ecclesiastes
Micah	2 Esdras (Ezra,		Song of
Nahum	Nehemiah)		Solomon

Habakkuk
Zephaniah
Haggai
Zechariah
Malachi

The Writings
Psalms
Proverbs
Job
Song of
   Solomon
Ruth
Lamentations
Ecclesiastes
Esther
Daniel
Ezra
Nehemiah
1 and 2
   Chronicles

Esther
Judith
Tobit
1, 2, 3, 4
   Maccabees

Poetical Books
Psalms
Odes
Proverbs
Ecclesiastes
Song of
   Solomon
Job
Wisdom
Ecclesiasticus
Psalms of
   Solomon

Prophetical Books
Hosea
Amos
Micah
Joel
Obadiah
Jonah
Nahum
Habakkuk
Zephaniah
Haggai
Zechariah
Malachi
Isaiah
Jeremiah
Baruch

Didactic Books
Job
Psalms
Proverbs
Ecclesiastes
Song of
   Solomon
Wisdom
Ecclesiasticus
Prophectical Books
Isaiah
Jeremiah
Lamentations
Baruch
Ezekiel
Daniel
Hosea
Joel
Amos
Obadiah
Jonah
Micah
Nahum
Habakkuk
Zephaniah
Haggai
Malachi

Books of Recent History
1 and 2
   Maccabees

Isaiah
Jeremiah
Lamentations
Ezekiel
Daniel
Hosea
Joel
Amos
Obadiah
Jonah
Micah
Nahum
Habakkuk
Zephaniah
Haggai
Zechariah
Malachi

> Lamentations
> The Letter of
> Jeremiah
> Ezekiel
> Susanna
> Daniel
> Bel and the
> Dragon

Do we then have an "official" form of the Old Testament which has something between one fifth and one quarter more material in it than the Hebrew Old Testament has?

The answer is yes—and no! Even here at this early stage we are already at a position in which the Apocrypha occupy a curiously elusive position, neither wholly Scripture nor wholly non-Scripture. Certain things have to be noted.

- There is never any word of an extension of the canon. The Greek writers knew and loved and used the Apocrypha, but they never at any time questioned the Hebrew canon of Scripture, and they never, as it were, listed any additions to it.

- The books included and not included in the Septuagint vary to some extent. For instance, 4 Ezra never occurs in the Septuagint, because, as we have seen, it does not exist in its Greek form. The Prayer of Manasseh is sometimes there and sometimes not there. Some manuscripts of the Septuagint contain 3 and 4 Maccabees, and sometimes a Psalm numbered Psalm 151. Even the number of the extra books is not strictly fixed.

- The great Jewish Alexandrian scholar was Philo. It was he who attempted to marry Jewish and Greek thought. He came from the area in which the Septuagint was born, although his work was done much later, just when the New Testament was coming into being. All his work is in the form of commentary on and exposition of Scripture. Philo knew and valued these extra books, but he never quotes them as Scripture.

• The writers of the New Testament were all Greek-speaking. Their Bible was not the Hebrew Old Testament; it was the Greek Septuagint. This was what they knew and quoted, but to all intents and purposes they never quote the books of the Apocrypha, and certainly not as Scripture.

Here there is the proof that the books of the Apocrypha occupied a curiously intermediate position, in which they were used and valued, and yet fell short of being in the full sense Scripture. One thing is noticeable about the use of these books, and even it has in it this double slant. As might be expected, we find in the early fathers two attitudes to these books. The fathers who were scholars and who knew Hebrew—and in the early times such scholars were few and far between—generally rejected the Apocrypha as Scripture and adhered to the Hebrew Bible, while the fathers who knew no Hebrew and who knew only Greek or Latin tended to accept the Apocrypha, because they found them bound into their version of the Old Testament. Thus Jerome and Origen, who were among the world's great scholars— Jerome had gone to reside in Palestine in order to learn Hebrew—were clear that the Apocrypha were not part of Scripture, while fathers like Tertullian and Augustine, who knew no Hebrew, accepted the Apocrypha as part of Scripture.

And yet the division was by no means as clear as that. Jerome could and did say, after listing the books in the Hebrew Old Testament: "Whatever is not included in this list is to be classed as apocryphal. Therefore Wisdom, commonly entitled of Solomon, the Book of Jesus the Son of Sirach, Judith and Tobit... are not in the canon." And yet, when it came to the point, at the request of the bishops he translated them and included them in the Vulgate, of which he was the translator and which became, and still is, the Bible of the Roman Catholic Church. As a scholar, Jerome would have banished the books of the Apocrypha; as a churchman he accepted them. As for Augustine, in his work *On Christian Doctrine* he included in the Old Testament Judith, Tobit, 1 and 2 Maccabees, Ecclesiasticus, Wisdom. He agreed with Jerome that they were not in the Hebrew Scriptures and that logically they should not be there, but he was worried about the effect of their exclusion on the minds of simple people who had long used and loved them. To him ecclesiastical tradition meant more than critical scholarship.

Origen was the same. About AD 240 Julius Africanus, the Bishop of Emmaus in Palestine, argued with him that Susanna is not in the Hebrew Bible and should not be regarded as Scripture. No one knew this better than Origen and as a scholar he would agree, but he argued that the Christian Church has always accepted these books for edification; he declared that the Church was not going to prune its reading to suit the Jews; he said that immemorial tradition was authority enough for reading these books. And he reminded Julius that the Bible itself said that ancient landmarks were not to be removed (Deuteronomy 19:14). There was always a tension between critical scholarship and Church tradition and tradition won. Rufinus introduced a distinction between *canonical* books and *ecclesiastical* books, and among the ecclesiastical books he included Wisdom, Ecclesiasticus, Tobit, Judith and 1 and 2 Maccabees. They were not canonical, but they were books of the Church. Jerome introduced still another distinction which stood for a long time, which in fact in some places stands even yet. He said of Ecclesiasticus and Wisdom that they are books which the Church reads "for edification of the people, but not for the proving of the doctrines of the Church."

So we see that in the early centuries for the Jews there was no question. Only the twenty-four books written in Hebrew were to be regarded as Scripture. In the Greek Old Testament, there were considerably more books. But the extra books in the Greek Old Testament were never quite reckoned as on the same footing as the Hebrew books. The Church knew them and the Church valued them and the Church would not abandon them, but it would not give them the same status as it gave to the Hebrew books of the Jewish Old Testament.

The Place of the Apocrypha in the English Bible

We now come to the place of the Apocrypha in the English Bible. In the earliest of the English Bibles, in Wycliffe's translation, the

Apocryphal books appear scattered throughout the Old Testament. This was so because Wycliffe did not translate from the Hebrew; he translated from the Latin Vulgate, and in the Wycliffe Bible the Apocrypha are as in the Latin Bible. But another influence was to weigh even more heavily on the English translators, and was to lead to the Apocrypha being given the position in the printed Bible, which they regularly occupy in the Protestant Bible. Luther's translation of the Bible into German was completed in 1534. It was not the Latin that Luther used; it was the original Greek and Hebrew. So in the Luther German translation the Apocryphal books are segregated into a separate section at the end of the Old Testament and before the New Testament. The section is headed: "APOCRYPHA—that is, books which are not held equal to the Holy Scriptures, and yet are profitable and good to read." Luther did not translate 1 and 2 Esdras (4 Ezra). He said of 2 Esdras (4 Ezra) that he threw it into the Elbe, and in his preface to Baruch he said of them that "they contain absolutely nothing which one could not find more easily in Aesop, or in even more trivial books." As far as the Protestant Church went, the position in the Bible that Luther gave to the Apocrypha became the standard position. When printed in the Protestant English Bible they regularly come between the Old and the New Testaments in a section of their own.

The first complete English Bible was that of Coverdale in 1535, and Coverdale followed Luther's example with certain slight differences. Coverdale printed a translation of 1 and 2 Esdras; he did not print the Prayer of Manasseh; and in his first edition he printed Baruch after Jeremiah. In the 1537 edition Baruch too was placed in the appendix with the rest of the Apocrypha; and the fashion was set. Coverdale's introduction to the Apocrypha is interesting:

> *These books (good reader) which be called Apocrypha are not judged among the doctors to be of like reputation with the other scriptures... And the chief cause thereof is this: there be many places in them that seem to be repugnant unto the open and manifest truth in the other books of the Bible. Nevertheless I have not gathered them together to the intent that I would have them despised, or little*

set by, or that I should think them false, for I am not able to prove it. Yea I doubt not verily, if they were equally conferred with the other open scripture (time, place and circumstance in all things considered) they would neither seem contrary, nor be untruly and perversely alleged. Truth it is: a man's face cannot be seen so well in a water as in a fair glass: neither can it be shewed so clearly in a water that is stirred or moved as in a still water. These and many other dark places of scripture have been sore stirred and mixed with blind and covetous opinions of men, which have cast such a mist before the eyes of the simple, that as long as they be not conferred with the other places of scripture, they shall not seem otherwise to be understood than as covetousness expoundeth them. But whosoever thou be that readest scripture, let the Holy Ghost be thy teacher, and let one text expound another unto thee. As for such dreams, visions and dark sentences as be hid from thy understanding, commit them unto God, and make no articles of them (i.e. base no doctrines on them). But let the plain text be thy guide, and the Spirit of God (which is the author thereof) shall lead thee in all truth.

Coverdale is, in effect, admitting the secondary character of the Apocrypha, and at the same time insisting that, properly used, they have their place and value.

The next date of note in the history of the Apocrypha in the English Bible is in the Bible of Thomas Matthew issued in 1537. It followed the custom of putting the Apocrypha by themselves between the Testaments, and it is notable in that it is the first English Bible to have in it the Prayer of Manasseh. Its version of the Prayer of Manasseh was translated from a French version, from Olivetan's Bible.

The next pronouncement regarding the Apocrypha was in the Geneva Bible. This Bible was made in Geneva by a band of English reformers who had fled from England when the persecution under Queen Mary threatened. Their leader was William Whittingham who was married to a sister of John Calvin. This is one of the most famous of all English Bibles, and not even the Authorized Version succeeded at first in displacing it. Between 1560, when it first appeared, and 1630 no fewer than about two hundred editions of the Geneva Bible, either as a whole or of the New Testament separately, appeared. It was the Bible of Shakespeare and of John Bunyan and of Cromwell's army and of the Pilgrim Fathers. The Geneva Bible was one of the great English Bibles. It had the Apocrypha in the now normal place between the Testaments, with one very odd exception. It placed the Prayer of Manasseh between 2 Chronicles and Ezra. In the table of contents it appears as "The Prayer of Manasseh, apocryphe." And a note in the margin of the prayer itself says: "This prayer is not in the Ebrewe, but is translated out of the Greke." Why the Prayer of Manasseh received different treatment from the other books of the Apocrypha is unknown. The Geneva Bible also makes its own pronouncement about the Apocrypha in general:

> *These books that follow in order after the Prophets unto the New Testament are called Apocrypha; that is, books which were not received by a common consent to be read and expounded publicly in the Church, neither yet served to prove any point of Christian religion, save inasmuch as they had the consent of the other Scriptures called canonical to confirm the same, or rather whereon they were grounded: but as books proceeding from godly men were received to be read for the advancement and furtherance of the knowledge of the history, and for the instruction of godly manners: which books declare that at all times God had an especial care for his Church and left them not utterly destitute of teachers and means to confirm them in the hope of the promised Messiah, and also witness that those calamities that God sent to his Church were according to his providence, who had both so threatened by his Prophets, and so brought it to pass for the destruction of their enemies, and for the trial of his children.*

Like their predecessors, the translators of the Geneva Bible saw the books of the Apocrypha as valuable, but valuable only within their limits.

In the Authorized Version the Apocrypha stand between the Testaments without note or comment. The assumption is that this is their place and no comment is needed. But Bruce Metzger points out one interesting fact about the Authorized Version and the Apocrypha. The Authorized Version had its marginal references, and they were relatively few, and in the Old Testament there were 102 references to the Apocrypha in the margin and in the New Testament 11. In the Authorized Version the Apocrypha are still an integral part of the whole.

It seemed that the books of the Apocrypha had established themselves as a kind of appendix to the Old Testament, and that they had acquired the status of honorable though not fully inspired books. But soon the situation was to change. Men's attitude to the Apocrypha became a thing of strong feelings.

There was opposition from Protestants on the ground that the Roman Catholic Church were the real possessors of the Apocrypha. It was possible by means of the Apocrypha to justify things which were abhorrent to Protestant belief. The Reformers would have nothing to do with them, if they could be cited to lend support to doctrines which to them were anathema. And on general grounds the Puritans were highly suspicious of documents, purporting to be sacred and inspired, which were extra to Scripture.

However, it is interesting to note an experience which Bunyan relates in his autobiography, *Grace abounding to the chief of Sinners.* About the year 1652 Bunyan went through a time of deep spiritual despondency. "One day," he says, "after I had been so many weeks oppressed and cast down, as I was now quite giving up the Ghost of all my hopes of ever attaining life, that sentence fell with weight upon my spirit, *Look at the generations of old and see: Did ever any trust in the Lord and was confounded?* At which I was greatly lightened and encouraged in my Soul; for thus at that very instant it was expounded to me: *Begin at the beginning of* Genesis, *and read to the end of the* Revelations, *and see if you can find that there was any that ever trusted in the Lord and was confounded.* So coming home I presently went to the Bible, to see if I could find that saying, not doubting but to find it presently; for it was so fresh, and with such strength and comfort on my spirit that I was as it talked with me." He goes on: "Well, I looked but I found it not. [This was in the days before concordances.] Only it abode upon me... Thus I continued above a year, and could not find the place; but at last casting my eye into the *Apocrypha* books I found it in *Ecclesiasticus* [2:10]."

So, Bunyan almost apologizes for finding anything helpful in the

Apocrypha! He goes on: "This, at the first, did somewhat daunt me; but because by this time I had got more experience of the love and kindness of God, it troubled me the less; especially when I considered that though it was not in those texts that we call Holy and Canonical, yet forasmuch as this sentence was the sum and substance of many of the Promises, it was my duty to take the comfort of it; and I bless God for that word, for it was God to me." "That word," he says, "doth still at times shine before my face." It is a most significant story, the story of a man who was almost afraid to be helped by the Apocrypha.

So at least in some quarters the tide was running against the Apocrypha, and the printers began to print the Bible without them. We can see that this began as a printer's doing for often we find the Apocrypha on the index page and we find the pages which should have been there with the Apocrypha missing, with a blank in the page numbering between the Old and the New Testaments. It became difficult to buy a Bible with the Apocrypha.

The trend is now different. The last sentence of the Introduction to the Apocrypha in the Revised Standard Version is a quotation of a sentence from Frank C. Porter: "Modern historical interest... is putting the Apocrypha in their true place as significant documents of a most important era in religious history." And the New English Bible includes an excellent modern translation of these books.

The Importance of the Apocrypha

Finally, we must ask, what then are we Bible readers to say about the Apocrypha? In his book *What Books belong in the Bible?* F. V. Filson puts the case strongly and convincingly for holding that the Apocrypha are no part of Scripture. He puts forward a series of arguments to prove his point of view.

- He is quite sure that they were never meant to be regarded as Scripture. At no time was there ever a canon of the Septuagint, the Greek Old Testament, as there was of the Hebrew Old Testament.

The number of extra books in the Septuagint was never laid down, and often varied. The extra books were never at any time given an official position as the books of the Hebrew Old Testament were. They are never at any time quoted by Jesus. They are never cited in the sermons of the early Church, for instance, in the sermons recorded in Acts. No one in the apostolic age ever quoted them as Scripture. The plain fact is that wherever Hebrew was known, it was the Hebrew Old Testament which was regarded as Scripture. In the early Church no one ever stated or even suggested that certain extra books had been added to the Old Testament. The place of these books in the Church was due only to use and practice. They were used, but they were never regarded as authoritative in the sense that the Hebrew books were so held to be.

- At no period in the history of the Church, even in the later days, were they ever unanimously and unquestioningly accepted, not even as we have seen in the Roman Catholic Church. There was always a doubt about them and a question mark against them. And books whose place has always been controversial cannot be part of the Scripture of the Church.

- They have nothing to add to the religious thought and belief of the Church. There is nothing in them that is not contained, and contained better, in the Old Testament. They have nothing to add to the books which were and are universally accepted.

- In the case of the books of the Old Testament, their inspiration is self-evidencing, but in the case of the books of the Apocrypha, this is not so. As Filson puts it, "we accept the Old Testament as Scripture by a personal and group confession that these writings, when brought home by the Holy Spirit, speak God's indispensable word to us with effective power." And it is precisely this that the Apocrypha do not do. The surest way to see the secondary character of the Apocrypha is simply to read them. To do so is to experience the difference between them and the books which are unquestionably Scripture.

Dr Filson will not even allow to these books a compromise position. "They are not Scripture," he says, "and they have no inherent right to a compromise position which practically treats them as Scripture while maintaining the fiction that they are without influence on doctrinal thinking."

But even if we hold that the apocryphal books have no claim to be regarded as Scripture, this is far from saying that we ought to, or can, completely discard them. They have an importance and a place.

- To begin with, they have a place in literature. They contain some of the world's great stories, and they are part of the literature of the world with which every properly educated person should be familiar. The Apocrypha have had their influence on literature and on music and on art.

In his chapter on "The Pervasive Influence of the Apocrypha" in his *Introduction to the Apocrypha* Bruce Metzger outlines this influence in many spheres, and quotes one surprising example of it. It was certain things said in the Apocrypha which sent Columbus out to discover America! A famous fifteenth-century writer called Pierre d'Ailly, who was a great scholar and Archbishop of Cambrai, wrote a book entitled *Ymago Mundi*, the *Image of the World*. In it there is a chapter *De Quantitate terrae habitabilis*, Concerning the Amount of Earth which is Habitable. On the basis of 2 Esdras (4 Ezra) 6:42, 47, 50, 52 he argued that six-sevenths of the earth is land and only one-seventh sea. The first passage reads: "On the third day you commanded the waters to be gathered together in a seventh part of the earth; six parts you dried up and kept so that some of them might be planted and cultivated and be of service before you." This made d'Ailly argue that since the earth is a sphere, and since only one-seventh is sea, the ocean between the west coast of Europe and the east coast of Asia can be "of no great width," and with a fair wind could be navigated in a few days. This is exactly what Columbus set out to prove. There was a copy of d'Ailly's book in Columbus' library, annotated in Columbus' own hand. It was this that sent Columbus voyaging, and it was this that at last persuaded hesitant sovereigns to Finance his expedition, for here was a sacred book which said that the sea covered no more than one-seventh of the earth, and could therefore easily be navigated!

- The Apocrypha have a place in the moral literature of the world. The moral advice given in Wisdom and Ecclesiasticus will never be out of date.

- The Apocrypha contain indispensable historical material, as for instance, the story of the struggle of the Maccabees for the freedom of the Jews.

- But the supreme use of the Apocrypha is that they bridge the gap between the Old and the New Testaments. In that gap there are three hundred years of which we will otherwise know very little. To move from the Old Testament to the New Testament is like jumping at one leap from the sixteenth to the nineteenth century. The great use of the Apocrypha is that they give us the political, cultural, ethical and religious background of the contemporaries of Jesus Christ, and therefore help us better to understand the New Testament.

The importance of the Apocrypha cannot be doubted and no student of the Bible can afford to disregard them.

4.

How to Study the Bible

*A*LL THROUGH THIS chapter I am going to assume that the person who wants to engage in the study of the Bible is a Christian, or at least wishes to be a Christian. We are to be thinking all the time of people whose desire it is to widen their knowledge and to deepen and enrich their Christian life and experience by the study of the Bible. We begin with the assumption of Arminius that, "The Church is that community which recognizes the word of God in the Scriptures."

The Bible, of course, must be studied as any other book is studied. To it we must bring all the rigor and the apparatus of scholarship. It must be approached with all the willingness to make an effort with which the student approaches the study of any of the world's great books.

But there is another side of this question which is no less important. If it is true that the Bible is to be studied with the *methods* with which any great book is studied, it is equally true that the Bible is not studied for the *purpose* for which any other book is studied. An ordinary book is studied for information, for instruction, for interest, for pleasure, as a textbook, as a task; but the Bible is written that in it the reader may find life and encounter God. In about AD 1000 Aelfric, one of the very early translators of the Bible, wrote a noble passage on what he felt the Bible to be:

Whoever would be one with God must often and often read the Holy Scriptures. For when we pray we speak to God; and, when we read the Bible, God speaks to us. The reading of the Scriptures produces a twofold advantage to the reader. It renders him wiser by informing his mind; and also leads him from the vanities of the world to the love of God. The reading of the Scriptures is truly an honourable employment, and greatly conduces to the purity of the soul. For as the body is nourished by natural food, so the sublimer man, that is, the soul, is nourished by the divine saying, according to the words of the Psalmist: "How sweet are thy words unto my taste, yea, sweeter than honey to my mouth." Happy is he, then, who reads the Scriptures, if he convert the words into actions. The whole of the Scriptures are written for our salvation, and by them we obtain the knowledge of the truth. The blind man stumbles oftener than he who sees; so he who is ignorant of the precepts of Scripture offends more frequently than he who knows them.

Read the Bible with Reverence

So then, in the very first place, readers must bring reverence to the Bible. Their duty will be to begin reading with prayer. Luther said of the student of Scripture that the "first duty is to begin with a prayer of such a nature that God in his great mercy may grant you the true understanding of his words." The Psalmist prayed: "Open my eyes, so that I may behold wondrous things out of your law" (Psalm 119:18), and we may well use the prayer that many of us know and love:

Blessed Lord, who hast caused all holy Scriptures to be written for our learning, grant that we may in such wise hear them, read, mark, learn, and inwardly digest them, that by patience and comfort of thy holy word, we may embrace and ever hold fast the blessed hope of everlasting life, which thou hast given us in our Savior Jesus Christ (Collect for Second Sunday in Advent.)

We will do well to take our thoughts back to the Jewish idea of the Spirit. As the Jew saw it, the Spirit of God does two things. First, the

Spirit brings God's truth to men and women. Second, and just as important, the Spirit enables them to recognize God's truth when they see it. This is to say that the same Spirit who moved the writers of the Bible to write their books is the Spirit who now enables us to study and to interpret these books.

We may see how the Spirit came to open the Bible to one of the greatest Christians of all time. Writing in 1545 Luther tells us how in his younger days he hated the very word *righteousness*. To him it always brought the idea that God in his righteousness is out to punish the unrighteous and the sinner. It was to him a word of terror. He never could understand the connection of the two halves of Romans 1:17: "For in it the righteousness of God is revealed through faith for faith: as it is written, 'The one who is righteous will live by faith.'" For days and nights he thought and meditated upon this text; and then he began to see that the word *righteousness* means that God in his mercy justifies man by faith. To put it very simply, he began to see that the righteousness of God is not the righteousness with which he threatens us, but *the righteousness which he offers us and gives us.* Then he writes:

> *At this point I felt completely reborn, and as if I had entered paradise with its open gate. In a moment the whole meaning of Scripture seemed to have changed. Thereafter I ran through the Scriptures as I had them in my memory, and collected analogical meanings in other words, such as the work of God, which means the work that God works in us, the virtue of God, which means the virtue through which he makes us powerful, the wisdom of God, which means the wisdom through which he makes us wise, the courage of God, the salvation of God, the glory of God. My love for that sweetest word* **righteousness of God** *was henceforth as great as my hatred for it had been hitherto. In this way this passage of Paul was truly the gate of Paradise.*

In one blinding flash of illumination the meaning of the passage had blazed upon him, and the meaning was not the way to knowledge but the way to paradise, when he saw that anything that is of God *is for* the man who has faith. To study the Scripture with reverence is the way to illumination by the continued action of the Spirit of God.

Let us take another example. Luther and Erasmus were two of the great figures of the Reformation, but they were very different. Erasmus was the grammarian, the philologist. He would identify the meaning of a word, disentangle the grammar of a passage—none could do so better—but there he left it. With theological definition he refused to become entangled. But Luther began where Erasmus left off. He asked, not only, What does this mean? but also, What does this mean *for me?* Erasmus had defined the meaning of *penitence*—it is "a change of mind and the understanding of one's own sin, after having suffered harm, and having recognized the mistake." There he left it, and there Luther took it up. Luther said—and said rightly—that such a change and such a recognition cannot take place "without a change of sentiment and love." A man's affections have to be set on different things, before he sees the error of the old things. Then Luther went on to say further—and rightly—such a change of sentiment and love can only be effected by the grace of God. A man cannot change himself—grace has to do that. So then Luther took the third step and declared that penitence is "a transmutation of mind and sentiment effected by grace"—and that, he said, is the translation of *metanoia,* penitence.

Here we have the difference. Erasmus approached the word penitence in the spirit of the man who would make a definition of it to grace a dictionary; Luther approached it in the spirit of the man who wanted to find salvation for his own soul, and for the souls of men and women. The grammarian and the theologian, the philologist and the evangelist—both are needed. But the really Christian study of Scripture approaches it in the attitude of that reverence which is seeking more than grammatical accuracy; it is seeking and finding the grace of God.

Study the Bible Within the Fellowship of the Church

The second rule for the study of Scripture is that it is best done within the fellowship of the Church. This does not mean ruling out Bible study on one's own. But the Second Letter of Peter lays it down: "First of all you must understand this, that no prophecy of Scripture is a matter of one's own interpretation" (2 Peter 1:20). To study Scripture wisely we must study it within the tradition of the Church.

To take the matter at its simplest this is the only sensible thing to do. If a man begins to study medicine, he does not start as if no one had ever studied medicine before. He enters into the discoveries and the works and the wisdom of all who went before. If a man embarks on the study of any branch of science, the first thing he does is to study the work that has been done on that part of the subject up until now. It would be a matter of folly—and arrogant folly at that—if when we came to the study of any passage of Scripture we completely neglected all that the scholarship and the devotion of the past had learned about it. It is an obvious fact that all learning begins in a fellowship of learning, and Christian learning should begin in the Christian Church. Luther said that the study of Scripture is only possible for a Christian. He held, and he held rightly, that to study any work profitably the experience of the reader must at least to some extent correspond with the experience of the writer. He held that it was a condition of any understanding of Scripture that the person who studies it must have a knowledge of Christ, since he, "the sun and truth in Scripture," is spoken of everywhere in the Bible, in the Old Testament as in the New. "The deeper the understanding of Christ," as Schwartz puts it in *Biblical Translation,* "the deeper the understanding of Scripture." Christians study Scripture both because they know Christ and want to know Christ.

Luther always held that Jerome's Latin Bible, the Vulgate, was not a good translation, because Jerome had produced it alone, and had thereby lost the promise that, where two or three are gathered together in his name, Jesus Christ is with them (Matthew 18:20). The study of the Bible in a Christian fellowship is richer than the study of the Bible in isolation and alone. (But see pages 150-51.)We have here three principles—First, no one can find the truth alone. Second, no human endeavor is effective without the Spirit and the grace of God. Third, no conclusion is valid, if it is arrived at having no regard for the fellowship of the Church.

Study the Bible Honestly

Students of the Bible must study the Bible honestly. This is to say, they must go to the Bible to find out and to seek the truth, and not to prove a case about which they have already made up their minds. It is common— it is almost usual—for people to use the Bible as an arsenal of proof texts to prove things about which they have already made up their minds. A man can use the Bible to find in it what he wants to find. He can use it to hear the echo of his own voice rather than the sound of the voice of God. Tyndale once said that the students who were taught by the priests and the monks came to the Bible "armed with false principles, with which they are clean shut out of the understanding of Scripture." Arminius once said: "Nothing is more obstructive to the investigation of the truth than prior commitments to partial truths." This is simply to say that not even God can teach a man who comes to the Bible with his mind made up.

F. C. Grant in *How to Read the Bible* tells how an ancient Rabbi once satirized his rival by saying: "When Rabbi Eliezer expounds, he begins by saying, 'Scripture, be silent, while I am interpreting." Hugh Pope in *English Versions of the Bible* quotes Gardiner as saying: "Scripture is a sweet, pure flower, whereof spiders gather poison and bees honey... Go thither instructed with wholesome doctrine and thou shalt see it confirmed. Go thither infected with malicious opinions and then thou shalt writhe out matter wherewith to maintain them." When we study the Bible we should be very sure that we are listening for God and not for the echo of our own voice.

Study the Whole Bible

If we are going to make the honest approach to Scripture, it specially means one thing. It means that our approach must be to *the whole of Scripture*. It is possible by making a selective approach to Scripture to argue in precisely opposite directions. If we quote Ecclesiastes 9:10: "Whatever your hand finds to do, do with your might; for there is no work or thought or knowledge or wisdom in Sheol, to which you are going," we can argue that there is no life after death. If we quote 1 Corinthians 15:19: "If for this life only we have hoped in Christ, we are of all people most to be pitied," we can argue that to remove the belief in a life after death is to cut the vital nerve of the Christian faith. If we quote the Old Testament law of an eye for an eye and a tooth for a tooth (Exodus 21:24; Leviticus 24:20; Deuteronomy 19:21) we can argue for the punishment of criminals by force, and, for instance, for the death penalty. If, on the other hand, we quote the command of Jesus to turn the other cheek and to love our enemies (Matthew 5:39, 44), then we can argue that purely retributory and vindictive punishment has no place in Christian society. If we quote Matthew 25:46: "And these will go away into eternal punishment, but the righteous into eternal life," we can argue that after death some go to eternal bliss and some to eternal hell by the judgment of God. If we quote John 12:32: "I, when I am lifted up from the earth, will draw all people to myself," we can argue for universal salvation.

There is nothing which so bedevils theological discussion as the one-sided and selective approach to Scripture, the approach in which a man quotes and cites that which suits his own point of view and agrees with his own case, and at the same time deliberately ignores all the material on the other side. That is why argument and discussion based on the quotation of texts can never get anywhere.

When we study Scripture we have to take the whole of Scripture to our problem and to our thought. We have to look at the matter, not in the light of any text or series of texts, but in the light of the whole mind and character of Jesus Christ as we know them, and in the light of the mind and heart of that God, who is the God and Father of our Lord Jesus Christ. An honest approach to the Bible is an approach to the whole Bible, and not a selection from the Bible to suit ourselves.

Study the Bible Wholeheartedly

Still further, and equally important, we have to take the whole of ourselves to the study of Scripture. Jesus said that we must love God with all our heart and soul and strength and mind (Luke 10:27), and that is the way in which we have to study the Bible.

There always have been some people who consciously or unconsciously left their minds behind them when they began to study Scripture. F. C. Grant in his book *How to Read the Bible* tells of an experience of a friend of his. His friend had been talking of how to study the Old Testament, and of how there are times when the Old Testament can be a difficult book. At the end of the talk a bright attractive young woman rose and said: "You don't need someone to tell you how to read the Bible. Open it anywhere, read three verses, make your mind a blank, and the Holy Spirit will do the rest!" The one thing you did not need, as she saw it, was intelligence; the one thing you did not need was your mind.

So then there is with some this suspicion of human reason, "the devil's whore," as Luther called it. But Luther was like so many great preachers who are men of passion and enthusiasm and conviction. He was very apt to stress one side of a question at a time, and it is often quite unsafe to regard anything he says as his final view of any subject, until you have checked up on the other side. Luther can argue—and argue rightly—that more than intellect is needed for the study of the Bible. He can and does argue that human and celestial wisdom are not the same thing. He can and does argue that it is not in human power, it is not in the scope of the human intellect, to understand the word of God. He can say: "Offer your empty heart to God, and the truth will be revealed."

Luther can certainly argue that the human intellect is quite inadequate to understand the word of God; he can certainly argue that a man's intellect may be his biggest handicap. "Reason is the devil's whore, and can do nothing but shame and disgrace everything that God does." "Faith strikes dead this reason, and kills this beast, which heaven and earth and all creatures cannot destroy." "Reason cannot rightly accord to God his deity nor attribute it to him as his own, though it rightly belongs to him alone. It knows that God exists. But who or what person it may be who is properly called God it does not know... Thus reason plays blind man's buff with God, and makes vain errors, and always misses the mark, calling God what is not God, and not calling God what is God." No one has ever spoken more contemptuously about human reason than Martin Luther.

But there is another side to this, and, when it is stated by Luther, the matter is perfectly reasonable. True, Scripture is given by the Spirit and can be understood only by the Spirit. It is only the author of Scripture who can interpret Scripture. "But the message of the Spirit is transmitted through language." "Words are the vehicles of thought; they are like the shrine in which God's truth is found." And there is need of the hardest kind of thought, the most intense kind of study, the most strenuous bringing to bear of the reason on the subject, to find the meaning of the words. This is where reason comes in. Reason has to be brought to bear on the givenness of the message of the Spirit. Devotion will grasp the message of the Spirit through grace; scholarship will toil at the meaning of the words in which the message is expressed.

So Melanchthon writes in the *Encomium Eloquentiae (In Praise of Eloquence):* "I have not the mistaken view that the holy can be penetrated through the industry of human talent. There is something in the holy that no one can ever see, unless it is shown to him by God: and Christ cannot be known to us without the Holy Spirit teaching us... But apart from prophecy, the meaning of words must be known, in which, as in a shrine, the divine mysteries are hidden. For what is the use of reciting in a magic way words that have not been understood? Is it not like telling a story to a deaf person?" The mind of man has to toil to understand and to communicate the message of the Spirit. Luther himself said that the Scripture teaches eternal life, and for that very reason it cannot be understood without the Spirit. Therefore we must pray to receive illumination, guidance and understanding. "But God will grant understanding only to him who perseveres in the study of words themselves, and meditates upon the meaning with which they are informed by the Holy Spirit."

The interaction between the Spirit of God and the mind of man is established. The Spirit helps the man who toils to help himself. God does not spoon-feed a man. The more a man brings to the Bible, the more he gets from it. When the grace and guidance of the Spirit meet the study, the toil and the endeavor of a dedicated mind, then indeed

Scripture opens its riches. A man has to bring the whole of himself—heart and mind—to the whole of Scripture.

Study of the Bible Leads to Action

One last general point concerning our attitude to Scripture must be noted before we turn to detail. The study of Scripture is meant to lead to action. We often hear of a *discussion* circle, but if the work of a circle ends in discussion there is something far wrong; it must end in action. J. A. Bengel had on his New Testament the famous two lines:

Te toturn applica ad textum;
Rem totam applica ad te.

This we may paraphrase: "Apply the whole of yourself to the study of Scripture; and then apply the whole of the result of your study to yourself."

And as Luther noted, in the last analysis it is not the regulations of a book with which we are dealing; it is the commands of a person, Jesus Christ. As Luther wrote in a letter to John Staupitz: "For thus do the commands of God become sweet, when we understand that they are not to be read in books only, but in the wounds of the sweetest Saviour."

When we study the word of God in a group, we should not do so for the sake of a pleasant argument and discussion; we should do so to find for ourselves the will of God, and having found it, we should not only know, we should also obey.

How to Study the Bible

We have spoken about the attitude of study. Let us now come to the actual technique of our study. We begin with one thing which must be clear. Our aim from beginning to end must be to find out what the Bible means. That sounds comparatively easy, but it is just here that the task of study has so often been complicated and wrongly conceived.

Allegory

The ancient Jewish scholars used to say that Scripture has four meanings. First, there is *Peshat,* the simple literal meaning. Second, there is *Remez,* the meaning by allusion, the meaning which the student can arrive at when he treats a passage not just as a straightforward narrative but as an allegory. Third, there is *Derash,* which means the homiletic application of the passage after it has been studied with all the aids to study available. And fourth, there is *Sod,* which is the inner meaning, the meaning to which only the spiritual expert can penetrate. *P*eshat, *R*emez, *D*erash, *S*od—note the initial letters of the words—P R D S. Hebrew has no vowels, only consonants; the vowels have to be specially inserted, and PRDS are the consonants of the Hebrew word for Paradise, and so the ancient scholars claimed that, if a student penetrated fully into these four meanings, he would be here and now in Paradise! But where they went wrong was that they neglected the simple, literal meaning, and went all out for the allegorical and the inner meanings, and once we start allegorizing Scripture we can make it mean anything.

Here is a comparatively simple example of how they allegorized. The passage is Ecclesiastes 9:14, 15:

> *There was a little city with few people in it. A great king came against it and besieged it, building great siegeworks against it. Now there was found in it a poor wise man, and he by his wisdom delivered the city. Yet no one remembered that poor man.*

That is a simple parable of the way in which people forget what has been done for them and are guilty of ingratitude. Now one of the basic beliefs of the Jews about human nature is that in every man there are two natures, the good nature and the bad nature; the good nature urges the man to goodness and the evil nature tries to seduce him into sin. So the Rabbis allegorized this parable. "There was a little city"—that is, the body. "With few people in it"—the few people are the limbs of the body. "A great king came against it"—that is the evil nature, the evil impulse. "Building great siegeworks against it"—the great siegeworks are the sins. "Now there was found in it a poor wise man"—that is, the good nature, the good impulse. "He by his wisdom delivered the city"—this means repentance and good works by which a man is saved. "Yet no one remembered that poor man"—because at the time the evil impulse holds sway the good impulse is altogether forgotten. Thus a simple story of ingratitude is turned into a complicated allegory of human nature.

Christian scholars for many centuries did exactly the same. The scholars of the Middle Ages had four Latin lines which spoke of the fourfold meaning of Scripture:

> *Litera gesta docet;*
> *Quid credas, allegoria;*
> *Moralis, quid agat;*
> *Quid speres, anagogia.*

The translation is:

> *The literal tells what happened;*
> *The allegorical, what you are to believe;*
> *The moral, what you are to do;*
> *The anagogical, what you may hope for.*

Schwartz *(Biblical Translation,* page 47) fills it out: "The literal sense explains the historical contents, the allegorical elucidates matters of faith by revealing the allegory contained in the biblical text, the moral sense indicates rules of human conduct, and anagogical sense deals with the future you may hope for (in the life to come)."

The trouble in the Christian approach to the Bible has often tended to be the way in which inner meanings were always being looked for in Scripture, and in which simple stories were given mystical meanings. The Greeks did this with Homer long before the Jews began doing it with the Old Testament. Take a Greek example. The Greeks had a god named Hermes. They then went on to derive *Hermes* from the Greek verb *erein,* which means *to speak.* Next they went on to say that Hermes is not meant to be taken as a person at all; he is a symbol, an allegory of the power of speech. They then went on to explain on these lines the various ways in which Hermes is described. He is called the *conductor,* because speech *conducts* one man's thoughts into his neighbor's soul. He is represented with *winged* feet, which stand for *winged words*. He is called *the leader of souls* because words soothe the soul to rest. He is called *the awakener from sleep,* because words rouse men to action. He carries a staff with serpents twined round it, and the serpents stand for the savage natures which are calmed by words (Edwin Hatch, *The Influence of Greek Ideas and Usages upon the Christian Church,* p. 63). So the god Hermes is allegorized into the power of speech.

The Jews did this regularly. Sarah and Hagar are the symbols of true wisdom and pagan philosophy. Lot's wife symbolizes the attachment of the soul to earthly things, an attachment which produces blindness to God and to his truth.

It is obvious that, if you treat Scripture like this, you can make it mean almost anything you choose. The most notorious example of this is Augustine's interpretation of the Parable of the Good Samaritan, which C. H. Dodd quotes in his book on the *Parables of the Kingdom* (Fontana Books, 1961, rev. edn).

A certain man went down from Jerusalem to Jericho; Adam himself is meant; Jerusalem is the heavenly city of peace from whose blessedness Adam fell; Jericho means the moon, and signifies our mortality, because it is born, waxes, wanes, and dies. Thieves are the devil and his angels. Who stripped him, namely, of his immortality . . . and left him half dead, because in so far as man can understand and know God, he lives, but in so far as he is wasted and oppressed by sin, he is dead; he is therefore called half-dead. The priest and Levite who saw him and passed by, signify the priesthood and ministry of the Old Testament, which could profit nothing for salvation. Samaritan means Guardian, and therefore the Lord himself is signified by this name. The binding of the wounds is the restraint of sin. Oil is the comfort of good hope; wine the exhortation to work with fervent spirit. The beast is the flesh in which He designed to come to us. The being set upon the beast is belief in the incarnation of Christ. The inn is the Church, where travellers returning to their heavenly country are refreshed after pilgrimage. The morrow is after the resurrection of the Lord. The two pence are either the two precepts of love, or the promise of this life and *of that which is to come. The **innkeeper** is the Apostle (Paul). **The supererogatory payment** is either his counsel of celibacy, or the fact that he worked with his hands lest he should be a burden to any of the weaker brethren (pages 13-14).*

If this is what the parable really means, it is obvious that no ordinary person could ever be expected to discover its meaning, and it is also obvious that there is no limit to the number of meanings that can be found in any passage of Scripture.

There is another famous instance of what allegorization can do in the Letter of Barnabas 9:7-9. Barnabas starts out from Genesis 17:23, 27. We there learn of the beginning of circumcision and that Abraham circumcised all the males in his household. By adding Genesis 14:14 to this we find that the number of them can be reckoned as *three hundred and eighteen.* In the Greek of the Septuagint, from which Barnabas is working, the number comes in the order *eighteen men and three hundred.* Now Greek has no figures for the numerals; the numerals are represented by letters of the alphabet, as if in English A were to equal 1, B were to equal 2, and so on. Well then, the Greek for *eighteen* is the letter *iota,* I, which stands for 10, and *eta,* the long Greek E, which stands for 8. That is to say, 18 is IÊ, which as anyone can see is the first two letters of the name IESOUS, which is Jesus. The Greek for *three hundred,* is the letter *tau,* T, and T is the shape of the Roman cross on which Jesus was crucified. So Barnabas says that *three hundred and eighteen* is IÊ, which stands for Jesus, and T which stands for the cross, and therefore when Abraham performed the first act of circumcision he did so "looking forward to the spirit of Jesus."

This is a fatal way of interpreting Scripture. It is a method which we should entirely avoid. The meaning for which we look is the meaning which the writer originally meant, not the meaning which later ingenuity can read into the text. To this day preachers often use allegorization, not it is true, with the perverted ingenuity with which the ancient interpreters used it, but in a more restrained way. That very great preacher, James S. Stewart, in his book of sermons, *The Gates of New Life,* has a sermon on Acts 27:29: "Then fearing lest we should have fallen upon rocks, they cast four anchors out of the stern, and wished for the day." He calls the sermon "Anchors of the Soul." He goes on to say that every soul should have four anchors—the anchors of hope, duty, prayer and the Cross of Christ. A simple action of sailors in the middle of a storm has been turned into an allegorization of the supports of the soul in the storms of life. The use of this method by even so great a preacher cannot justify it for us. It is the original meaning of Scripture that we must set out to find.

The Original Meaning of Scripture

If our primary task is to find out the meaning of Scripture, then the beginning of our study must be the study of words. We take only two illustrations of how illuminating the study of words can be.

Three times Paul speaks about the *earnest of the Spirit*. The word for earnest is *arrabôn*. *Arrabôn* is a word from business and commercial Greek. An *arrabôn* was the part of a purchase price or a contract price, paid in advance, as a guarantee that the full price would in due time be paid. So a woman sells a cow, and gets so much as *arrabôn* in guarantee that the full price will be paid. A man engages a mousecatcher. Mice did a great deal of harm in the vineyards at harvest time, and he pays him so much as *arrabôn,* so that he will begin on the extermination of the pests straight away. A group of castanet dancing-girls are engaged for a village festivity and they are at once paid so much as *arrabôn,* as a guarantee that the full contract price will be paid after they have performed. An *arrabôn* was a first installment of the full purchase price, and a guarantee that the full purchase price would be paid. So Paul speaks of the Holy Spirit as God's *arrabôn.* This is to say that for the Christian the gift of the Spirit is the first installment of the life of heaven, and the guarantee that some day that heavenly life in all its fullness will come.

Very commonly the Holy Spirit is called the Comforter. In the Authorized Version in John's Gospel Comforter is the title and description of the Holy Spirit (John 14:16, 26; 15:26; 16:7). There are few things which have so limited and truncated the real work of the Holy Spirit as the consistent use of this word "Comforter." The word in Greek is *Paraklêtos,* which is sometimes transliterated into English in the form Paraclete, as in the hymn, "Come, thou holy Paraclete."

The Greek word *paraklêtos* literally means *someone who is called in to the side of some one else.* In Greek the meaning of the word is always decided by the purpose for which the person is called in. It may mean someone called in to give evidence for the defense, a witness in favor. It may mean someone called in to plead one's cause, an advocate for the defense. It could mean someone summoned to render medical aid, a physician. It is used to describe someone speaking to the men of a depressed and dispirited army, who by his words and the impact of his personality puts fresh strength and courage into them.

It can be seen from these examples that a *paraklêtos* is someone who is called in to help one who is in difficulties to cope with the situation. So then the Holy Spirit is the person through whom there come to us the strength and grace of God to enable us to cope with life. Certainly, part of this work is to comfort, but only part. To call the Holy Spirit the Comforter, and to stop there, is to have a limited and rather sentimental view of the Spirit, whereas in the Greek the word is full of power and of the promise of the God-given ability to face and to master any situation in life.

How then did this word Comforter get into the English translation of the Bible? It came in with Wycliffe about 1386, and it has stayed ever since. But in the days of Wycliffe it was a perfect translation. The word *comfort* is derived from the Latin word *fortis,* which means *brave,* and originally the word meant someone who puts courage into you. Let us take two other examples of it in Wycliffe. Wycliffe translates Ephesians 6:10, "Be ye *comforted* in the Lord." And he translates 1 Timothy 1:12, "I do thankings to him who *comforted* me." In both cases the word in the Greek is *endunamoun,* whose root word is *dunamis,* power, from which the word *dynamite* comes. In Wycliffe's day to *comfort* a person was to fill that person with a power like spiritual dynamite. The Holy Spirit does not simply come and wipe our tears away; he gives us a dynamic power to cope with life.

So then the first step in the technique of the study of the Bible must be to ascertain the meaning of the passage which is being studied, and that study must start with the investigation into the meaning of words. This means that, ideally speaking, a Bible study group should be led by someone who knows the original languages, Hebrew and Greek. This will be an obviously impossible demand. Failing that,

the group should have access to someone who possesses such knowledge. But even that is an impossible demand. The assumption would
be that the minister of the Church would be such a person, but modern methods of ministerial training do not necessarily include training
in the original languages. So the group will probably need to depend
on the use of commentaries which have been made for English readers
and which are in English, but which are founded on the original languages. Some such commentaries are listed at the back of the book.

The Need for a Modern Translation

Our search for meaning will bring us to another necessity. If we are
to ascertain the meaning of any passage of Scripture, we shall need to
use a modern translation. The Authorized Version is a version which
will always be known and loved as one of the supreme achievements
of the English language, but there are at least three reasons why, from
the point of view of study, it is now an inadequate translation.

Change in the Meaning of Words

There are passages in it which have now ceased to be intelligible to
modern ears, or in which the meaning of words has altered. The astonishing thing in a translation made in 1611 is not that such things exist in it,
but that on the whole there are so few. Here are some examples of that.

> *They **fetched a compass** of seven days' journey. (2 Kings 3:9)*

> *From thence we **fetched a compass** and came to Rhegium. (Acts 28:13)*

To fetch a compass means to make a circuit.

There is in the Authorized Version a now abandoned and often
misleading use of the word *prevent*.

> *The sorrows of hell compassed me about; the snares of death **prevented** me. (Psalm 18:5)*

> *Why did the knees **prevent** me? or why the breasts that I should suck? (Job 3:12)*

*In the morning shall my prayer **prevent** thee. (Psalm 88:13)*

*The inhabitants of the land of Tema brought water to him that was thirsty, they **prevented** with their bread him that fled. (Isaiah 21:14)*

In modern English the word *prevent* means to hinder, to impede, to stop a person doing something; in the language of 1611 it meant to go before, to precede, and therefore to meet or to encounter, but with no thought of hindrance, or prevention in the modern sense of the term.

There is a still more misleading use of the word conversation.

*Ye have heard of my **conversation** in time past in the Jews' religion. (Galatians 1:13)*

*Be thou an example of the believers, in word, in **conversation**, in charity, in spirit, in faith, in purity. (1 Timothy 4:12)*

*Who is a wise man and endued with knowledge among you? let him show out of a good **conversation** his works with meekness of wisdom. (James 3:13)*

*Be ye holy in all manner of **conversation**. (1 Peter 1:15)*

*Having your **conversation** honest among the Gentiles. (1 Peter 2:12)*

In modern language a man's *conversation* is the way in which he talks; it is his speech, his language, his thought. But the word *conversation* comes from the Latin *conversari*, which means to walk up and down, to go to and fro, and it therefore means, not his talk, but his whole conduct and behavior. In all these instances we have quoted it is not a question of being careful of our talk, but of being careful of our whole behavior, of our whole life and conduct. The last instance is doubly deceiving. In it *honest* does not mean telling the truth. In 1611 the word *honest* far more commonly meant *honorable*. And so 1 Peter 2:12 really means: "In your contact with the Gentile world see that your conduct is always honourable."

It is quite clear that in our search for meaning we need a translation which speaks the language not of the seventeenth but of the twentieth century.

The Archaic Language of the Authorized Version

There is another characteristic of the Authorized Version which it is relevant to note. The great characteristic of the Authorized Version is the beauty of its English, and this beauty is accompanied by a certain archaism. The language is beautiful, but the language is not the language of the twentieth century, and it is precisely this combination of beauty and archaism which gives the Authorized Version the solemnity and the dignity which are dear to so many. Now a translation should reproduce not only the meaning of the original but also the atmosphere of the original.

In the case of the Old Testament the atmosphere of the Authorized Version is not at fault, for the Hebrew of the Old Testament is for the most part classical Hebrew, Hebrew at its best. But in the case of the New Testament the matter is very different. The Greek of the New Testament is colloquial Greek; it is the kind of Greek that people spoke on the street in the first century. It is not classical Greek. We have noted that, even if the New Testament were to lose all its religious importance, it would still have a unique importance in that it is the only written monument of that colloquial spoken Greek of the first century. Now here is the point—the more solemn and dignified and beautiful and archaic a translation of the New Testament is, the worse a translation it is. The New Testament in translation should not sound beautiful and dignified and solemn and old; it should sound modern, colloquial, the kind of language people speak in their homes and on the street, the kind of language they read in their newspapers. In the case of the New Testament a solemn, dignified, archaic translation could not be a worse translation, for that is all that the New Testament Greek is not.

Any translation of the New Testament ought to speak to a man in the vernacular in which he speaks; any other kind of translation is a bad translation.

So then in 1611 the Authorized Version was a good translation—but not now. When Luther spoke about his own translation of the Bible, he said that it was not to those who spoke Latin that the translator must go. "We must ask the mother in the home, the children on the street, the common man in the market-place about this, and look them in the mouth to see how they speak, and afterwards do our translating." The first essential of a New Testament for use in the study of its meaning is a New Testament in the language of our own generation.

The Inaccuracy of the Authorized Version

The third fact about the Authorized Version is the most serious of all. It is obvious that no translation can be better than the manuscripts on which it is founded. Before printing was invented manuscripts were of course copied by hand. Even with the most careful copying by hand new errors crept in with each successive copying. Therefore, the older a manuscript is the more correct it is likely to be. The nearer it is to the original, the fewer removes there are between it and the author's original writing, the more accurate it will be. Further, the more manuscripts there are available, the more likely it is that in some of them the original readings will be preserved.

The Authorized Version was published in 1611. It was made from a Greek text, in the case of the New Testament, which was largely that of Erasmus, revised by Beza and Stephanus. This Greek text was based on not more than ten Greek manuscripts, of which the earliest was not earlier than the tenth century. This is to say, that the Authorized Version is a translation of a Greek text of the New Testament which is quite inadequate. This was not the fault of the translators; nor was it the fault of those who constructed the text which was used. They used the best that was available in 1611. But since then all kinds of discoveries have been made and many new manuscripts have come to light. We have now available manuscripts which go back to the third and fourth centuries, and the manuscripts which are now available can be numbered by the score and even by the hundred. This is to say that in the twentieth century there are available manuscripts which are up to seven or eight hundred years older than the manuscripts which were the basis of the Greek text from which the Authorized Version was translated, and there are hundreds more of them.

Much as we love the Authorized Version as a monument of English prose, much as we rest our hearts in its music and in its cadences, we cannot do anything other than recognize that in the twentieth century it is no longer an adequate translation. This is not to say that we are to stop reading the Authorized Version for spiritual and devotional purposes; but it is to say that it can no longer be properly used as the basis of real Bible study. For the purposes of study we must use translations such as the Revised Standard Version, the Jerusalem Bible, the New International Version or the Revised English Bible. To refuse to make the change is to shut our eyes deliberately to the new knowledge of his word which God in our day and generation has made available for us.

The Background of Biblical Passages

When we have established the meaning of the passage, so far as the actual wording goes, the next task is to put the passage into its context and into its background. It is impossible to understand a person without understanding something about his background. It is, for instance, impossible to understand why a person is what he is, until we know something about his home and his parents and how he was brought up. So it is important to know *that* a thing happened; it is even more important to know *why* it happened; and to know this it is necessary to know the context and the background of the event. Let us take two examples of this, one from the area of geography and one from the area of life and customs.

One of the supreme differences between modern and ancient times is the annihilation of distance. A man may nowadays breakfast in London and lunch in New York over three thousand miles away. The world today is a small place, and the life people live today is a mobile life. Jesus, however, in his life in Palestine was never, as far as we know, more than a hundred miles from home. When we read the Samuel story in the first two chapters of 1 Samuel it seems that Hannah and the boy Samuel are very far apart. Once a year she goes to see him and takes with her the little coat that she had made for him. The journey has all the atmosphere of an expedition, and yet in fact Ramah, where Hannah lived, and Shiloh, where the child Samuel served, were about seventeen miles apart! Take the case of the Flood in Genesis 6. There the Flood is told of in terms of a world event. But for the writer of that story the world is Mesopotamia and the Euphrates Valley. America, Africa, Australia, Britain—the ancient writer had no conception that these continents and countries even existed. To him the world was that small part of it he knew: we must not think that the word *world* meant to him a world in which three thousand miles is a morning's journey.

Take a more detailed example—Jesus' cleansing of the Temple. The cleansing of the Temple is one of the most terrifying stories in the Gospel history. The idea of the white hot anger of Jesus, the picture of the Jesus with the whip, are frightening conceptions. Let us then see first of all where this incident happened. It happened in the Court of the Gentiles. The Temple in Jerusalem was composed of a series of courts, and the entry into each court was increasingly limited. Into the Court of the Gentiles, anyone, Jew or Gentile, might come. Next came the Court of the Women beyond which no women could go. Between it and the Court of the Gentiles there was a low wall, into which there were inset stone tablets warning any Gentile that to proceed beyond this wall was a crime for which the penalty was instant death. Beyond the Court of the Women was the Court of the Israelites beyond which no layman could go. Finally there was the Court of the Priests in which were the great altar, and the seven-branched candlestick and the table of the showbread, and the altar of the incense, and into it only the priests could go. At the far end of the Court of the Priests stood the Holy Place and the Holy of Holies, into which only the High Priest could go and that on the occasion of the Day of Atonement only. So then the farther into the Temple the various courts went, the fewer people were allowed into them. And this incident of the cleansing of the Temple happened in the one area of the Temple into which a Gentile might come. If Gentiles were to worship and pray in the Temple at all, here alone they might do so.

Next, who are the characters involved? First, there are the money-changers. Every male Jew and proselyte—women and minors were exempt—had to pay a Temple tax of one half-shekel per year. A half-shekel was the equivalent of about seven pence. But this must be evaluated in the light of the fact that a working man's daily wage averaged about four pence. The tax was near enough two days' pay—which is quite something. Further, this Temple tax had to be paid in either sanctuary shekels or Galilean shekels. This was so because these were the only coins which had no king's head on them, and a coin with a king's head was for a Jew a graven image, especially since so many kings were given divine honor. For all ordinary purposes in Palestine any coinage would do and was valid—Greek, Roman, Phoenician, Egyptian, Syrian and so on. The tax was paid at Passover time, and people came from all over the world to keep the Passover and to pay their tax. With them they brought all kinds of money. They were bound to pay. Within Palestine, if a man did not pay, the Temple authorities could and did distrain upon his goods. So the pilgrims went to the money-changers to have their money changed into the right kind of shekels. For every coin changed the changers charged one *maah*, which was the equivalent of one penny, and, if the coin presented was larger than a half-shekel and change had to be given, another *maah* was charged for giving change—and remember a *maah* was the equivalent of the quarter of a day's pay. So the pilgrim had to pay his tax which was the equivalent of nearly two days' pay, and, he might well have to pay another half day's pay to get his coin changed and to receive his change. It was one colossal racket in which poor pilgrims were being mercilessly fleeced. It brought in between £8,000 and £9,000 a year, which in modern terms would be millions, and such was the wealth of the Temple treasury that, when Crassus, the Roman general, plundered it in 54 BC, he took away the equivalent of two and a half million pounds, and that did not exhaust it. The modern purchasing power of such a sum would be in the category of hundreds of millions of pounds. The pilgrims were being victimized by the money-changers.

The others involved were the pigeon-sellers. Almost all the visitors to the Temple would make some offering or other, and for the poorer people the commonest victim was the pigeon or the dove. A sacrificial victim had to be without spot or blemish, and the Temple authorities had appointed inspectors to see that victims were perfect. It was possible for a pilgrim to buy pigeons outside the Temple; there were shops where they were on sale. But all the likelihood was that the inspector would find a blemish. So it was safer to buy the victims at the Temple shops where they had already been inspected. Outside the Temple a pair of pigeons could cost as little as two pence, but inside the Temple they could cost as much as seventy-five pence. Here was a still more lucrative racket and the shops in the Court of the Gentiles, where the trading went on, were called the Bazaars of Annas.

So then we see why Jesus was enraged. Poor pilgrims were being fleeced. The one place where Gentiles could worship was turned into a shouting, arguing, bargaining oriental market. And we can see why Annas and company hated Jesus; their vested interest had been attacked. Put into its background, the cleansing of the Temple becomes vividly meaningful.

In so far as it is possible every Bible incident should be read against its background. This often means work and research in order to understand—but the result is worth it.

The Importance of Poetry in the Bible

Another important point for interpretation is that there are parts of the Old Testament which are poetry and to treat them as prose is to misunderstand them and to do them injustice.

We take one outstanding example of that, Joshua 10:12, 13:

> *On the day when the Lord gave the Amorites over to the men of Israel, Joshua spoke to the LORD; and he said in the sight of Israel,*
>
> > *"Sun, stand still at Gibeon,*
> > *and Moon in the valley of Aijalon."*
> > *And the sun stood still, and the moon stopped,*
> > *until the nation took vengeance on their enemies.*

This is clearly a passage at which we would have to look with some care, in order to arrive at a correct interpretation of it. The first thing that strikes us about it is that it cannot in any event be taken literally for the very simple and sufficient reason that the sun does not in fact move; the sun always stands still. It is the earth which moves, and if at any time the earth had ceased to move, then life as we know it would have come suddenly and catastrophically to an end. Further, if anything resembling this had somehow or other happened, if there had been an occasion when it could be said that the sun or the earth stood still, then this would be an event, not simply of Jewish history, but also of world history, and there would be some record or memory of it in the history of every nation in the world. It is not possible to approach this with a crude literalism.

But then we note something else about it. It is a quotation from the Book of Jashar (Joshua 10:13). This Book of Jashar is quoted again. It is quoted as the origin of David's great lament over the death of Saul (2 Samuel 1:18). And so the fact becomes clear that the Book of Jashar is in fact a book of poetry, and the material that is in it is poetry. The New Revised Standard Version prints the Joshua story as poetry and correctly so.

So then in this passage we have a poet speaking. The poet here speaks of the sun in the same kind of way as the poet of Psalm 19, who speaks of the sun daily leaving his chamber like a bridegroom and running his daily race from one end of the heavens to the other (Psalm 19:5, 6). This is the language of poetry; it is even the language we use in everyday life. We say of an occasion: "It was the longest half hour that I spent in all my life," but all half hours are thirty minutes, neither more nor less. We say of a golden day: "Never did the time pass more quickly," but the time always passes at the same rate.

So we need not worry trying to find explanations of the Joshua passage. It means that by the help of God that day was long enough for the victory to be won, that into it there were by the grace of God packed these events which gave victory to God's people Israel. We do the Bible an ill service when we turn the beauty of its poetry into prose.

The Bible as Developing Revelation

We come now to what may well be the most important single thing to remember when we are seeking to interpret the Bible. It took all of one thousand years to write the Bible, and the period of history covered in the Bible—apart from the parts of the Bible which deal with the things which happened before history can be said to have begun— amounts to something like three thousand years. Take one thousand years in modern terms. Go back a thousand years and we arrive somewhere about the time of Alfred the Great. Clearly, life and thought and society and civilization were very different one thousand years ago. It is so with the Bible. If the Bible story stretches over scores of centuries, there cannot be in it one flat level of thought and religion and ethics. There is bound to be development. God could only tell men what men were able and willing to receive. God's message to men had to be adapted to the state of men's minds when that message was given. If we are going to teach a boy algebra, we do not start with the binomial theorem; we lead slowly up to it. If we are going to teach a child to play the piano, we do not start with Bach's preludes and fugues; they are a summit, not a beginning. If we are going to teach a boy Greek, we do not start with the odes of Pindar, or the choruses of Aeschylus; something much easier has to be the beginning. It is so with the Bible. God had to lead the minds of men from less to more, from lower to higher levels, from the glimmerings to the full blaze. This is obvious, for, if men knew it all already, why should the great prophets come, and above all why should Jesus come? Revelation is an ongoing process all the time.

Very commonly this is called the principle of *developing revelation.* God's revelation, so to say, developed with man's ability to receive it. It would be better to speak, not of a *developing revelation,* but rather of a *developing grasp of revelation.* It is not so much that God doled out his revelation in small doses; it is rather that he was offering the blaze of truth all the time, but the mind of man was capable of and willing to receive only a limited amount of it.

When we find in the Bible things which are sub-Christian, there is no need to defend them, and there is no need to explain them away. They represent the stage which men had reached at that particular time. This we know, because Jesus more than once said: "You have heard that it was said . . . But I say to you" (Matthew 5:21, 27, 31, 33, 38, 43). We accept this in practice, for there are few or no Christians who live out all the ceremonial laws of the Old Testament. We know that with Jesus Christ these have been left behind. It is not that they were wrong; it is not that they were in error. But that they were incomplete. Behind every one of them there is a great and unchanging truth, and these old laws are imperfect grasps of that truth. They represent what men made of that truth at that particular stage. We can see this in many things in the Bible, but we shall illustrate it, first, by looking at certain religious practices, and, second at certain religious principles in which there has been development.

Religious Practices

Let us look first at the answer to the question, *How do I show my religion?* as that question is answered in the legal parts of the Old Testament.

Dietary laws

The Jew showed his religion by abstaining from certain kinds of food. As everyone knows the Jew would not, and will not, eat pigs' flesh:

> *The pig... is unclean to you. Of their flesh you shall not eat, and their carcasses you shall not touch; they are unclean to you. (Leviticus 11:7, 8)*

That is laid down as a law in Leviticus, but it does not stop us eating bacon for breakfast, or a pork chop for dinner.

Phylacteries and the mezuzah

The Jew showed his religion by wearing the tasselled cloak, the phylacteries or prayer boxes, and by putting the *mezuzah,* the little cylindrical wooden fixture with words of Scripture in it on his doorpost; the phylacteries were little leather boxes with certain texts written in parchment inside them, and were strapped to the wrist and the forehead at prayer:

> *The Lord said to Moses: Speak to the Israelites, and tell them to make fringes on the corners of their garments... You have the fringe so that, when you see it, you will remember all the commandments of the LORD. (Numbers 15:37-39)*

> *Keep these words that I am commanding you today in your heart... Bind them as a sign on your hand, fix them as an emblem on your forehead [phylacteries], and write them on the door-posts of your house and on your gate [**mezuzah**]. (Deuteronomy 6:6-9)*

The Jew still wears his tasseled prayer shawl and his phylacteries at prayer; he still fixes the *mezuzah* to the door of his house or flat. But the

Christian does not consider these commandments in any way binding.

Circumcision

Above all the Jew showed his religion by circumcision. This was the sign of the covenant. This was the sign that he was a member of the people of God. So important is it that it is said:

> *Any uncircumcised male who is not circumcised in the flesh of his foreskin shall be cut off from his people; he has broken my covenant. (Genesis 17:14)*

But no Christian accepts the obligation of circumcision.

The Jew shows his religion by abstention from certain foods, by the wearing of certain objects and by affixing certain things to his house and by circumcision. Let no one belittle these things; they are a public demonstration of the faith of the Jew, and it would be a good thing if Christians showed their faith as openly. But this is the way in which a Christian shows his religion:

> *By this everyone will know that you are my disciples, if you have love for one another. (John 13:35)*

In the Old Testament there are ways of showing a man's religion—and they are honorable ways. They grasp the fact that man must show his faith, but they have not reached the full revelation that a man must show his faith by his love. This had to wait for Jesus.

Enemies of God

Next, let us look at the answer to the question, *How do I protect my religion?* How do I keep it safe from any infection which would make it less pure?

It is in the answer to this question that we find some of these things which fill us with horror as we read. In the event of war if a city surrenders, then its inhabitants are to be put to forced labor.

> *If it does not submit to you peacefully, but makes war against you, then you shall besiege it; and when the LORD your God gives it into your hand you shall put all its males to the sword. You may, how-*

ever, take as your booty the women, the children, livestock, and everything else in the town, all its spoil... But as for the towns of these peoples that the LORD your God is giving you as an inheritance, you must not let anything that breathes remain alive. You shall annihilate them. (Deuteronomy 20:12-17)

The instructions are followed at the siege of Jericho and the result is:

Then they devoted to destruction by the edge of the sword all in the city, both men and women, young and old, oxen, sheep and donkeys. (Joshua 6:21)

In the war with Amalek Samuel's instructions from God to Saul are:

Now go and attack Amalek, and utterly destroy all that they have; do not spare them, but kill both man and woman, child and infant, ox and sheep, camel and donkey. (1 Samuel 15:3)

It sounds and it is so bloodthirsty. But what must be remembered is this—in this there was no personal hatred, there was no blood lust, there was no murderous passion for slaughter. What was behind it was this—all foreign faiths were an infection; they were a threat to the purity of the worship of Jahweh; and everything to do with them had for safety's sake and for purity's sake to be wiped out. This is actually said, for the instructions in Deuteronomy conclude with the words which give the reason for all this:

That they may not teach you to do all the abhorrent things that they do for their gods, and you thus sin against the LORD your God. (Deuteronomy 20:18)

The whole point is that these foreign nations were idolaters, and were therefore the enemies of God, and therefore had to be wiped out lest the infection of their heathen practices taint the purity of Hebrew religion.

But when Jesus comes, we get a new conception. We get the conception that we are not to wipe out God's enemies by killing them; we are to wipe them out by converting them. In the American civil war over slavery Abraham Lincoln was charged with being far too gracious and kindly to the southern states. "They are your enemies," people said to him, "and it is your task to destroy them." Lincoln answered: "Do I not destroy my enemies when I make them my friends?" The Old Testament had got hold of half of a great truth, the truth that the enemies of God must be destroyed. But we have to wait for Jesus to discover that the way to destroy the enemies of God is to convert them so that they become the friends of God.

Sacrifice and Offerings

The third question which it is natural to ask is, *What is it that I ought to give to God?* What gift can I take to him to please him?

There is a great part of the Old Testament which is all about the sheep and lambs and calves and bulls and oxen and doves and pigeons and wine and flour and oil which form part of the ceremonial sacrifices to God. The theory behind this is quite dear. The worshipper says to himself: "I must give to God my most precious possession," and in an agricultural society his most precious possession was the animals and the crops over which he had toiled.

But even in the Old Testament itself the inadequacy of this is seen. Isaiah hears God say:

> *What to me is the multitude of your sacrifices?*
>   *says the LORD;*
> *I have had enough of burnt offerings of rams*
>   *and the fat of fed beasts;*
> *I do not delight in the blood of bulls,*
>   *or of lambs, or of goats.*
> *When you come to appear before me*
>   *who asked this from your hand?*
>   *Trample my courts no more;*
> *Bringing offerings is futile;*
>   *incense is an abomination to me . . .*
> *Wash yourselves; make yourselves clean;*
>   *remove the evil of your doings*
>   *from before my eyes;*
> *cease to do evil,*

> *learn to do good;*
> *seek justice,*
>   *rescue the oppressed,*
> *defend the orphan,*
>   *plead for the widow. (Isaiah 1:11-13, 16-17)*

As Isaiah saw it, the whole paraphernalia of sacrifice was one vast irrelevance. Micah said the same:

> *With what shall I come before the LORD,*
>   *and bow myself before God on high?*
> *Shall I come before him with burnt offerings,*
>   *with calves a year old?*
> *Will the Lord be pleased with thousands of rams,*
>   *with ten thousands of rivers of oil?*
> *Shall I give my first born for my transgression,*
>   *the fruit of my body for the sin of my soul?*
> *He hath told you, O mortal, what is good;*
>   *and what does the Lord require of you*
> *but to do justice, and to love kindness,*
>   *and to walk humbly with your God? (Micah 6:6-8)*

And it is in Hosea that we find what looks as if it was Jesus' favorite text:

> *For I desire steadfast love and not sacrifice. (Hosea 6:6;*
> *Matthew 9:13; 12:7)*

It is clear God never wanted the sacrifice of animals. The Jews thought he did, because they saw in these animals their most precious possessions, and to God they were willing to give them. But the prophets saw the irrelevance of animal sacrifice, and Jesus above all saw it. The most precious thing a man has is his heart, his self, a heart and a self filled with love for God and love for man—that is the only gift God wants.

So in the Old Testament we see time and time again that a great truth is grasped, but it is imperfectly grasped. For the full grasp we have to wait for Jesus. It is not that the Old Testament is wrong—far from that; it is an essential stage to that goal which is Jesus Christ.

Religious Principles

Let us now take two of the very great conceptions of the Christian faith and let us see how they develop throughout the Bible, until they culminate in Jesus Christ.

First, let us take the conception of *the forgiveness of our enemies and of those who have injured us.*

Unlimited Vengeance

In the beginning so far from any desire to forgive there was a cry for unlimited vengeance. Genesis 4:23, 24 is one of the oldest fragments in the Bible, and in it the cry is for vengeance:

> *Lamech said to his wives:*
> *"Adah and Zillah, hear my voice;*
> *you wives of Lamech, listen to what I say:*
> *I have killed a man for wounding me,*
> *a young man for striking me.*
> *If Cain is avenged sevenfold,*
> *truly Lamech sevventy-sevenfold."*

It is Lamech's boast that he has exacted vengeance for injury. He has killed a man for injuring him, and his desire is for a vengeance which will exceed the injury seventy-sevenfold. Here in the most primitive of all passages there is no thought of forgiveness, only for vengeance.

Precise Retribution

The next stage is a stage at which the Old Testament has often been, and still is, much misunderstood. It is often said that the Old Testament believes in "an eye for an eye, and a tooth for a tooth," and this is claimed to be one of "the bloodthirsty laws of the Old Testament."

> *If any harm follows, then you shall give life for life, eye for eye, tooth for tooth, hand for hand, foot for foot, burn for burn, wound for wound, stripe for stripe. (Exodus 21:23-25)*

Anyone who maims another shall suffer the same injury in return: fracture for fracture, eye for eye, tooth for tooth; the injury inflicted is the injury to be suffered. One who kills an animal shall make restitution for it, but one who kills a human being shall be put to death. (Leviticus 24:19-21)

Show no pity; life for life, eye for eye, tooth for tooth, hand for hand, foot for foot. (Deuteronomy 19:21)

To call these bloodthirsty laws is totally to misunderstand them; they are the precise reverse of that.

In the early days the vendetta or blood feud was typical of tribal society. In the vendetta, if any man injured a member of another tribe, it was the duty of all the members of the injured man's tribe to take all possible vengeance on all the members of the tribe of the man who injured him. And thus a comparatively slight injury could lead to a war between two tribes in which many lives were lost. These laws which we have just quoted were the first attempt to *limit* vengeance. If vengeance was to be taken, it must be only to the precise extent to which injury had been inflicted, and no longer must injury issue in a bloodthirsty tribal war.

In later times this law of precise retribution became modified. Suppose a man's tooth is knocked out, and the tooth is a decayed tooth, it will be unjust to knock out in retribution a tooth which is a healthy tooth. Suppose the eye which was injured to be a very inefficient eye, it will be wrong to knock out in revenge a perfectly healthy eye. So each injury came to be assessed at a money penalty, and not as a physical exchange of injuries. But the main point is that here there is the first step towards the controlled limitation of vengeance, and it is therefore a very big step in the right direction.

Conditional Forgiveness

At the third stage we arrive at a stage when forgiveness and non-retaliation are urged, but with certain limitations and for certain conditions.

• Forgiveness is urged, with the limitation that it is to extend only to fellow Hebrews.

You shall not hate anyone of your kin in your heart; you shall reprove your neighbour, or you will incur guilt yourself. You shall not take vengeance nor bear a grudge against any of your people, but you shall love your neighbour as yourself; I am the LORD. (Leviticus 19:17, 18)

This is definite enough but the forgiveness is limited to "your kin," and to "any of your people." It does not necessarily extend to the Gentile.

- Forgiveness is urged, because vengeance belongs to God, and if a man's cause is just, he can leave the vengeance to God:

Do not say, "I will repay evil."
Wait for the LORD, and he will help you. (Proverbs 20:22)

The same attitude is seen in the inter-testamental book *The Testament of the Twelve Patriarchs:*

Love one another from the heart; and if a man sins against you, cast forth the poison of hate and speak peaceably to him, and retain no guile in your soul. And if he confesses and repents, forgive him... And if he is shameless and persists in his wrong-doing, even so forgive him from the heart, and leave the avenging to God. (The Testament of Gad, 6:3, 7)

True, forgiveness is urged, but God will exercise the vengeance for the good man.

- Most commonly of all, forgiveness is urged in order to win the favor of God:
  If your enemies are hungry, given them bread to eat,
  and if they are thirsty, given them water to drink;
  for you will heap coals of fire on their heads,
  and the LORD will reward you. (Proverbs 25:21)

  Do not rejoice when your enemies fall,
  and do not let your heart be glad when they stumble;
  or else the Lord will see it and be displeased,
  and turn away his anger from them. (Proverbs 24:17, 18)

Even a passage like Lamentations 3:30,

To give one's cheek to the smiter, and be filled with insults,

derives from the fact that:

The Lord is good to those who wait for him, to the soul that seeks him. (Lamentations 3:25)

It is the same with a passage from Ecclesiasticus 28:2:

Forgive your neighbour the wrong he has done,
and then your sins will be pardoned when you pray.

So again:

If anyone seeks to do evil to you, do good to him, and pray for him, and then you shall be redeemed by the Lord from all evil. (The Testament of Joseph, 18:2)

One of the few Old Testament passages on forgiveness in which there is no limitation and no conditions is Proverbs 24:29:

Do not say, "I will do to others as they have done to me;
I will pay them back for what they have done."

So then the Old Testament begins with unlimited vengeance; it moves on to a strictly controlled exchange of penalty; it moves still further on to the urging of forgiveness, but within certain limits and conditions.

Absolute Forgiveness

And so finally we come to Jesus. The essence of the teaching of Jesus on forgiveness is in the Sermon on the Mount:

You have heard that it was said, "An eye for an eye and a tooth for a tooth." But I say to you, Do not resist an evildoer. But if anyone strikes you on the right cheek, turn the other also... You have heard that it was said, "You shall love your neighbour and hate your enemy." But I say to you, Love your enemies and pray for those who persecute you, so that you may be children of your Father in heaven; for he makes his sun rise on the evil and on the good, and sends rain on the righteous and on the unrighteous. For if you love those who love you, what reward do you have? Do not even the tax collectors do the same? And if you greet only your brothers and sisters, what more are you doing than others? Do not even the Gentiles do the same? Be perfect, therefore, as your heavenly Father is perfect. (Matthew 5:38-48)

There are no limitations and no conditions. Forgiveness is absolute. There is a reward, but the reward is that he who forgives becomes like God. As Paul put it:

Be kind to one another, tenderhearted, forgiving one another, as God in Christ has forgiven you. (Ephesians 4:32)

So the wheel has gone full circle; it began with unlimited vengeance and it ends in Christ with unlimited forgiveness. (Contrast Christ's seventy times seven, Matthew 18:22, with Genesis 4:24.) On this matter we have to say unequivocally, "It is not by the Old Testament but by the New Testament, not by the Law but by the Gospel, not by anyone other than Jesus Christ, that I judge my duty to forgive." So when people quote the Old Testament to us, we have to say quite frankly, "This is the stage which at that time men had reached. This is the part of God's revelation which they had grasped. But the full revelation is in Jesus Christ, and we take our orders and our pattern from no one but him."

Life After Death

The second great idea at which we must look is *life after death*. We shall look at the development of that idea throughout the Bible.

Sheol

In the earliest times the Hebrews had no real belief in any life after death. They believed that the souls of all who died went to Sheol or Hades. Sheol is not hell; Sheol was the place of all the dead. It was a grey, shadowy land, from which all the color and the strength and the meaning had been evacuated. It was separated from man and from God alike, and the souls who lived there lived a ghostly, spectre-like existence. It was not extinction, but it was no more than the shadow of life. Again and again this hopelessness comes out in the Old Testament.

> *For in death there is no remembrance of you;*
>   *in Sheol who can give you praise? (Psalm 6:5)*

> *What profit is there in my death,*
>   *if I go down to the Pit?*
> *Will the dust praise you?*
>   *Will it tell of your faithfulness? (Psalm 30:9)*

> *Turn your gaze away from me, that I may smile again,*
>   *before I depart and am no more! (Psalm 39:13)*

> *For my soul is full of troubles,*
>   *and my life draws near to Sheol.*
> *I am counted among those who go down to the Pit;*
>   *I am like those who have no help,*
> *like those forsaken among the dead,*
>   *like the slain that lie in the grave,*
> *like those whom you remember no more,*
>   *for they are cut off from your hand . . .*
> *Do you work wonders for the dead?*
>   *Do the shades rise up to praise you?*
> *Is your steadfast love declared in the grave?*
>   *or your faithfulness in Abaddon?*
> *Are your wonders known in the darkness,*
>   *or your saving help in the land of forgetfulness? (Psalm 88:3-12)*

> *The dead do not praise the LORD,*
>   *nor do any that go down into silence. (Psalm 115:17)*

> *For the fate of the humans and the fate of animals is the same; as one dies, so dies the other. They all have the same breath, and humans have no advantage over the animals; for all is vanity. All go to one place; all are from the dust, and all turn to dust again. (Ecclesiastes 3:19, 20)*

> *Whoever is joined with all the living has hope, for a living dog is better than a dead lion. The living know that they will die, but the dead know nothing; they have no more reward and even the mem-*

ory of them is lost... Whatever your hand finds to do, do with your might; for there is no work or thought or knowledge or wisdom in Sheol, to which you are going. (Ecclesiastes 9:4-10)

For Sheol cannot thank you,
death cannot praise you;
those who go down to the pit cannot hope
for your faithfulness. (Isaiah 38:18)

For there is hope for a tree,
if it is cut down, that it will sprout again,
and that its shoots will not cease.
Though its root grow old in the earth,
and its stump dies in the ground,
yet at the scent of water it will bud
and put forth branches like a young plant.
But mortals die, and are laid low;
humans expire, and where are they?
As waters fail from a lake,
and a river wastes away and dries up,
so mortals lie down, and do not rise again;
until the heavens are no more they will not awake,
or be roused out of their sleep. (Job 14:7-12)

It is clear that in the Old Testament there is little to hope for after death—a land of shadows, a land of the dark, a land of silence, a land of forgetfulness, a land which is cut off from God and from men. J. E. McFadyen wrote in *The Message of Israel* (p. 46): "There are few more wonderful things than this in the long story of religion, that for centuries men lived the noblest lives, doing their duties and bearing their sorrows, without hope of future reward; and they did this because in all their going out and coming in they were very sure of God." Then McFadyen went on to say: "An American scholar has said that 'it has never been possible for man, thinking man, on a basis of *this life only,* to make life anything but meaningless nonsense.' The Old Testament is the triumphant refutation of such an assertion." In the earliest form of Hebrew religion there was no belief in any real life beyond the grave and on the other side of death.

The Possibility of Life after Death

But this is not the end of the matter in the Old Testament. In the Old Testament there are many passages which are at least on the way to a belief in life after death. Isaiah can say:

> *Your dead shall live, their corpses shall rise.*
> *O dwellers in the dust, awake and sing for joy!*
> *For your dew is a radiant dew,*
> *and the earth will give birth to those long dead. (Isaiah 26:19)*

In Daniel we find the belief:

> *Many of those who sleep in the dust of the earth shall awake, some to everlasting life, and some to shame and everlasting contempt. Those who are wise shall shine like the brightness of the sky; and those who lead many to righteousness, like the stars forever and ever. (Daniel 12:2, 3)*

Let us trace the process and the reasons by which the real belief in life after death came into being.

The Universal God

The greater men's conception of God, the more they came to be certain that there was no part of the universe outside the being of God. When men thought of their God as only the god of their nation, and when they were willing to grant that each nation had its own god, then the area of God's power was strictly limited; but when they moved on to believe in only one God, the God of all men and all nations and all possible worlds, then they could not avoid thinking of him also as the God of that world which came after death.

> *Where can I go from your spirit?*
> *Or where can I flee from your presence?*
> *If I ascend to heaven, you are there!*
> *If I make my bed in Sheol, you are there! (Psalm 139:7, 8)*

Once men began to believe in one God of all the universe, then this life and any other life are in the presence of God, and the idea of Sheol was bound to change.

A Leap in the Dark

Sometimes men's glimpse of a life to come was like a leap in the dark. It was not a settled belief to begin with. It was something which a man grasped like a life-belt in a sea of trouble. It was that way with Job. We have already quoted Job's words of despair, and Job could despair:

> *As the cloud fades and vanishes,*
> *so those who go down to Sheol do not come up. (Job 7:9)*

But Job felt that it would make all the difference in the world if he could only hope for something. As Galloway once said: "The enigmas of life become at least less baffling, when we come to rest in the thought that this is not the last act of the human drama." So Moffatt translates Job's hope:

> *If only man might die and live again,*
> *I could endure my weary post until relief arrived;*
> *thou wouldst call, and I would come,*
> *when thou didst yearn for life that thou hadst made.*
> *(Job 14:14, 15)*

So in Job's heart there was the longing—if only there was something still to come! And then suddenly he makes the leap:

> *I know that my Redeemer lives,*
> *and that at last he will stand upon the earth;*
> *and after my skin has been thus destroyed,*
> *then in my flesh I shall see God,*
> *whom I shall see on my side,*
> *and my eyes shall behold, and not another. (Job 19:25-27)*

It is not a settled doctrine; it is not a reasoned faith; it is not part of a creed. It is the first leap in the dark to grasp at God, not just in this life, but for ever.

The Relationship with God Was Unbreakable

Sometimes the belief in the life to come came not from any sudden leap, but from the growing conviction that a relationship, a connection, a friendship, a link established with God is in its essence unbreakable, just because God is God. So the man who had found God in this world believed that, since God is always God, you cannot lose him. To say that love is immortal would mean the same thing. So the Psalmists wrote:

> *Nevertheless I am continually with you;*
> *you hold my right hand.*
> *You guide me with your counsel*
> *and afterward you will receive me with honour.*
> *Whom have I in heaven but you?*
> *And there is nothing on earth that I desire other than you.*
> *My flesh and my heart may fail,*
> *but God is the strength of my heart,*
> *and my portion forever. (Psalm 73:23-26)*

> *I keep the Lord always before me;*
> *because he is at my right hand,*
> *I shall not be moved.*
> *Therefore my heart is glad, and my soul rejoices;*
> *my body also dwells secure.*
> *For you do not give me up to Sheol,*
> *or let your faithful one see the Pit.*
> *You show me the path of life;*
> *in your presence there is fullness of joy,*
> *in your right hand are pleasures for evermore. (Psalm 16:8-11)*

In these two passages there is the confidence of a heart which has established a connection with God which it is convinced cannot be terminated by death.

The Life to Come and the Justice of God

But perhaps that which most of all brought to the Hebrews a real belief in a life to come was simply the fact that, unless they brought another world into the scheme of things, then neither God's promises to the nation nor to the individual would ever be fulfilled. There was a time when men looked for God's rewards and punishments within this present time scheme. The Psalmist said:

I have been young, and now am old;
  yet I have not seen the righteous forsaken,
  or their children begging bread. (Psalm 37:25)

But it became less and less possible to say that. The good man might die in agony in the cruelty of the persecutor. The man of principle was so often—as he still is—the man the world hates. Israel was the chosen people, but Israel was a nation subjugated by the Assyrians, the Babylonians, the Persians, the Greeks, the Romans. The plain fact was that without a life to come it was impossible to believe in either the love or the justice of God. In the famous phrase, the new world was called in to redress the balance of the old. Thus between the Testaments this belief in a life to come became strong, so that those who had been true to God might find their reward and that the promises of God might yet be fulfilled.

They that fear the Lord shall arise to eternal life; their life shall be in light, and it will never cease. (Psalms of Solomon 3:12)

After that, when the time of the Advent of the Messiah is completed, he shall return in glory into the heavens. And then shall all those arise who slept with their hope in him. (Apocalypse of Baruch 30:1)

Since God's man never received God's blessing in this distressful life, men were driven to believe in the life to come.

The Certainty of Life to Come

But at the best this was a hope, and not until the coming of Jesus does the hope turn to certainty. It is the word of Jesus:

In my Father's house there are many dwelling places. If it were not so, would I have told you that I go to prepare a place for you? And if I go and prepare a place for you, I will come again and will take you to myself, so that where I am you may be also... Because I live, you also will live. (John 14:2, 3, 19)

As Paul sees it, the Christian certainty of the life to come comes from the fact that the Christian's Savior is one who was dead and is alive again:

As all die in Adam, so all will be made alive in Christ.
(1 Corinthians 15:22)

In Jesus Christ what had been a hope became a certainty, and what
had been a theory became a fact. And so within the Bible we see the
belief in the life to come developing from the gray shadowy Sheol to
life for ever with the Lord. And once again, when people quote the
grim parts of the Old Testament where belief in the life to come does
not in any real way exist, then we do not need to defend these parts,
and we do not need to explain them away. Once again we can say,
"Yes, that is as far as men had reached at that time. But that is not the
Christian belief. These are only steps on the way to the conviction of
life in Christ here and hereafter."

The Bible Writers

There is one more big demand on us in our study of the Bible. To
understand any book we have to try to enter into the mind and the
heart and the life and the circumstances of the person who wrote it.
We have to try to see how his mind works; we have to try to understand his general world view. This is just as true of the Bible as of any
other book. We must try to enter into the mind of the people who
wrote it. To go to the Bible with the eyes and the ideas and the pre-
conceptions of a twentieth century Western man is the surest way to
misunderstand it. We have to try to think ourselves into the mind of a
man of the date at which each book was written. And we have continually to remind ourselves what the object of the writers of the Bible
was in writing at all. Their one object was to show the ways of God
with men; their one aim was to show life in terms of the sovereignty
of God. Their aim was exclusively religious. They were not writing
history; they knew no more of scientific history than any of their contemporaries did. They were not writing science; their science was as
rudimentary as that of their age. Their aim was to show God in
action.

There is nothing at all unnatural in this. A man is always an expert within an area. My mother knew no Hebrew and no Greek and no theology, but she was the greatest saint I ever knew. I would never have gone to her for the translation of a word or for the expounding of a doctrine; but I would have gone to her every time to learn how to live with God as a constant companion. So in the Bible I do not look in the first place for history; I do not look at all for science; but I do look for God—and I find him. Let us then see some of the things which we must remember, if we are to enter into the minds of the biblical writers.

Their View of the World

They have a quite different view of the world. For them the earth was the fixed center of things, and the sun emerged each day to run his daily race across the heavens (Psalm 19:4, 5). The earth is like a flat plate sitting on the waters with the solid dome of the firmament over-arching it, across which the great lights of the sun and moon traveled and which opened for the waters above to make the rain (Genesis 1:1-19). But the important thing is not what they believed the earth to be like; the important thing is what they believed humanity to be like, and what they believed God to be like, and that they were quite certain that, whatever the earth is like, the creating power of God is behind it.

Sickness

They have a quite different view of sickness. They attributed sickness to the demons or to the sin of the sick person. It was not only mental illness that they ascribed to the demons. Any part of the body might, as they thought, be occupied and rendered ill by a demon. All illness, so they believed, had some sin behind it.

We no longer attribute illness to the demons or necessarily to the sin of the sick person himself. But in one way these ancient thinkers were curiously modern. What we have been saying is that, in the modern term, they believed illness to be psychosomatic. *Psuchê* is the Greek for *soul,* and *sôma* is the Greek for *body.* And to say that illness is psychosomatic means that it has more than a physical cause; it has its spiritual causes as well. It may indeed have no physical cause, only a physical effect. This means that it is never enough to concentrate on man as a body, but that he has a spirit as well, and the body will never be healthy until the spirit also is whole. Healing, and in their own way the ancient writers saw this, is always more than a physical matter.

Pictorial Thought and Demythologizing

They have quite a different way of thinking, and this is the most important and the most difficult point of all. Among the Hebrews in biblical times there were few—perhaps none—who thought, or could think in abstract terms and abstract arguments. *They thought in pictures.* Now, the pictures in which they thought were bound to be the pictures of their own time, the pictures which were part of the scene of day-to-day living in their own day, for the simple reason that these were the only pictures which the people of their day could understand. So, then, inevitably what happens to us is that we are confronted with a piece of timeless truth enclosed in a quite local and temporary picture. And time and time again our task is to penetrate beyond the husk of the picture to the kernel of the truth.

This process has a name—and it is a name which very unfortunately and very unfairly has become to many people a bad word. It is called *demythologizing.* The trouble about this is that the word *myth (muthos)* means one thing in Greek and another in English. In English a myth is a piece of fiction, and to say that a thing is mythical is well nigh the same as to say that it is untrue. But in Greek a myth is a story designed to make clear some truth which it is difficult or impossible to put into plain language which an ordinary man can follow. A myth is truth in a picture.

Time and time again our task in studying the Bible is to get at the timeless truth at the back of the temporary picture. The twentieth century scholars were far from being the first to recognize this need. Origen, the great scholar, knew all about it and stated it clearly and forcibly half-way through the third century *(De Principiis, 1:16):*

What man of sense will suppose that the first and the second and the third day, and the evening and the morning, existed without a sun and moon and stars? Who is so foolish as to believe that God like a farmer planted a garden in Eden, and placed in it a tree of life, that might be seen and touched, so that one who has tasted of the fruit by his bodily lips obtained life? Or again, that one was partaker of good and evil by eating that which was taken from a tree? And if God is said to have walked in a garden in the evening, and Adam to have hidden under a tree, I do not suppose that anyone doubts that these things figuratively indicate certain mysteries, the history being apparently but not literally true... Nay, the Gospels themselves are filled with the same kind of narratives. Take, for example, the story of the Devil taking Jesus up into a high mountain to show him from thence the kingdoms of the world and the glory of them: what thoughtful reader would not condemn those who teach that it was with the eye of the body—which needs a lofty height that even the near neighbourhood may be seen—that Jesus beheld the kingdoms of the Persians, and Scythians, and Indians, and Parthians, and the manner in which their rulers were glorified among men?

Origen begins by noting that in the creation story it is three times said that there was evening and morning *before the* sun and moon were created (Genesis 1:5,8,13,14). What Origen is saying is that here we have truth, but truth in a picture. The picture is the husk; the truth is the kernel. Let us take briefly the three stories to which Origen refers.

The Creation Story

There is the creation story, or rather there are two different creation stories. If you ask any intelligent schoolboy to put into one sentence what Genesis 1 and 2 are saying, he will at once answer: "They are saying that God made the world." That is the answer. The *method* by which he made it is not in question. The *fact* that God's creating power is behind this universe and is responsible for this universe is the kernel, however that creating power was exercised.

The Fall of Man

There is the story of the Fall in Genesis 3. This story is in fact the story of *the fall of every man*. It is worthwhile noting that the name Adam is not a proper name at all; it is in fact the Hebrew word for *man*. This is everyman's story. The man who wrote it would not even know that there was such a word as *psychology*, but there never was written a story more psychologically true than this one. Take it step by step.

• God gives a command.

• There comes the temptation to break it. Sin always implies that we know better than God; it is putting our wish above God's will.

• The wrong thing is attractive (verse 6). It looks good; it was good to eat; to take it would be to win something apparently well worth while. Sin is always attractive. If I can only have this, I will be happy.

If the forbidden thing was ugly and repulsive, there would be no power in temptation. Temptation has power, because the forbidden things look attractive and desirable and profitable.

• Sin is committed and the first instinct is to hide (verse 8). No sooner have we committed a sin than we want to hide it from others, to hide it from God, and, if possible, to refuse to look at it ourselves. And there is no greater folly than thinking that anything can be hidden from God.

• When confronted with sin, our first instinct is to push the blame on to some one else. Adam said: "Don't blame me; blame Eve." Eve said: "Don't blame me; blame the serpent." The sinner blames everyone but himself.

Genesis 3 is a story which was never meant to tell of something which happened in a moment of time. It is the story of what happens to Adam—to man—to every man—to you and to me.

The Temptation of Jesus

Finally, let us take the story of the temptations of Jesus (Matthew 4:1-11; Luke 4:1-13). Origen was right; there is one thing which should make us stop and think—there is no mountain from which anyone can literally see all the kingdoms of the world. Jesus had gone out into the desert to decide how he was to do the task God had given him to do. Was he to use the way of force, of material things, of sensations, of compromise—or the way of the Cross? All that this story tells was not happening visibly and externally. It was going on in the mind of Jesus. He was fighting the battle with all that was trying to lure him from the way God wanted him to take. If you had seen him during it, you would have seen a man alone—or not alone—with God. Just as temptation comes to us, so it came to him, not physically, visibly, but with the attack in the mind and in the heart.

Always we have to remember as we read the Bible that we are reading the work of men who thought in pictures. We must never waste time in argument about whether this is literally and physically true or not. It is spiritually for ever true, and beyond the husk of the story we must find the kernel of truth—and live by it.

There are just three things more to say about reading and studying the Bible.

• While we should study the Bible in detail, we should often, to get the best of it, read it in long sections. We should, for instance, read Mark's Gospel at a sitting, and see the four-act drama—preparation, conflict, tragedy, triumph—opening before us. It is possible sometimes to spend too much time on detail and too little on the panoramic and the dramatic picture of the whole.

• However long and however devotedly we study the Bible, there will still be passages which are too difficult and which we cannot understand. A man once came to Spurgeon complaining that there were parts of the Bible he did not understand, and saying that he had stopped reading it. Spurgeon said: "When I am eating a nice piece of fish and come upon a bone, I don't fling the whole fish away; I put the bone at the side of the plate and leave it there; and I go on enjoying the fish." When we come to something in the Bible that, even after study, we still do not understand, then we can leave it and pass on. The day will come, when we may understand; and for the present there is wealth enough and more to be going on with.

• One last thing—there is everything to be said for regular and systematic reading of the Bible. In his autobiographical study... *And Another Thing,* Howard Spring tells how he got the habit. It was during the war in 1940, when things were at their worst. He went to his desk to work, and he found that he could not concentrate for thinking of the threat to our country. It so happened that very recently someone had given him a copy of Marcus Aurelius' *Meditations.* He picked it up and began to read, and somehow the gallant and astringent Stoic philosophy did something to him. "Thereafter," he said, "I made a practice of beginning the morning not by sitting down at my desk with a mind inflamed by all the surging incertitude of the times, but by standing up and reading erect for half-an-hour or so from Marcus Aurelius. I found it a salutary and strengthening custom... In this way I read twice through the *Meditations,* and by then it seemed to me that no day should be begun with a plunge straight into 'business,' whatever that business might be. A few moments of quietness in the company of a supreme and tranquil mind seemed to pay dividends that would make a company promoter lick his chops. It is so easy to begin the day with a rush through the morning paper and a rush through the morning mail, and then to make a rush at the work in hand, but I now think so foolish and so unnecessary. It is like playing the fiddle before it has been keyed up; it will be off pitch all day." But Howard Spring did not stop there. He goes on: "After the second reading of the *Meditations,* I began the mornings with readings from the Bible, and it was during these readings of a book neglected for a quarter of a century that the central importance of a loving God and love of the brethren took possession of my mind."

Howard Spring found that that daily reading brought a serenity and a strength into life, and through it God took possession of his mind. We too ought to be regular in reading the Bible. Howard Spring, being an author, could do his work at home, and was not the slave of the clock. It may be that for us with a train to catch and an office to get to and a family to live among the morning reading will not be possible, or will at least be very difficult. But the reading can just as well be the last thing at night, and we can go to rest thinking of God and of his ways with men.

If we adopt this method of regular reading, it will not be the best of plans to begin at the beginning of the Bible and to go on to the end. We will be far better to use a carefully prepared scheme of daily readings with comments. In that way our reading will be guided and directed; the difficulties will be explained; the meanings will be brought out; and we will have the sense of being one of a great company reading with us all over the world. To read the Bible with system and with help is the way to get the best out of it, for thus we will get strength for the way, wisdom for our minds, and the love of God for our hearts.

5.

The Inspired Book

WHAT EXACTLY DO we mean when we say that the Bible is inspired? Or, to put it in another way, what do we mean when we say that the Bible is the word of God? This is not a question which it is easy to answer, but it is a question which Christians must face, because on their answer to it depends the place which they will give to the Bible in their life and belief.

It is not difficult to prove that the Bible is a unique book, with a unique effect on the lives of men and women. We shall take two examples of that. When Sir Walter Scott was dying, he asked his son-in-law Lockhart to read to him. Lockhart, thinking of the many books that Sir Walter had written and of the great library at Abbotsford, lined from floor to ceiling with thousands of books, asked: "From what book shall I read?" And Scott answered: "Need you ask? There is but one." At the moment of the twilight of life and the dawn of eternity there was only one possible book.

One of the most famous Bible stories in the world is the story of Tockichi Ishii. Ishii was a Japanese criminal with a unique record of savage murder. He was a man of fiendish brutality, pitiless as a tiger. He had callously murdered men and women and even little children. He was captured and condemned and he was in prison awaiting execution. He was visited by two Canadian women. They could make no impression on him; he would not even speak or answer; he simply glowered at them like a wild beast. In the end they had to go, but they left a Bible with him. For some reason Ishii began to read the book, and, when he started, he could not stop. He read on until he came to the story of the Cross. It was the saying of Jesus: "Father, forgive them; they know not what they do," that broke him. "I stopped," he said. "I was stabbed to the heart, as if pierced by a five-inch nail. Shall I call it the love of Christ? Shall I call it his compassion? I do not know what to call it. I only know that I believed, and the hardness of my heart was changed." When in the end the jailer came to lead him to the scaffold, instead of the surly, hardened, brutal, almost beastlike man he once had been, he went to death with a serene, smiling, gentle radiance, for Tockichi Ishii the murderer had been reborn by reading the word of God.

The Bible as the Literal Word of God

Events like these leave us in no doubt that this book is unique. We describe that uniqueness by saying that this book is inspired, that it is the word of God. But what do we mean by that?

The answer has sometimes been given that this book was written by God; that every word and syllable and letter, every page and paragraph and sentence is the writing of God; that the book is the verbatim word of God. That view is the basis of what is called verbal inspiration. As a theory of inspiration it goes very far back. On this theory the men who wrote the Bible had no more to do with what they were writing than the pen in an author's hand or the typewriter on which this chapter is being typed. In Whittingham's New Testament, the precursor of the famous Geneva Bible, the name of Paul is—rightly—not attached to the Letter to the Hebrews, and there is a note to point out that "seeing the Spirit of God is the author thereof, it diminishes nothing the authority, although we know not with what pen he wrote it." The author, whoever he was, was on this view no more than a pen in the hand of God.

Athenagoras wrote of "God moving the mouths of the prophets like musical instruments." He spoke of the Spirit using the writers as a flute-player breathes into a flute (*Embassy,* 7 B, 9 D). Justin Martyr speaks of the divine Spirit coming down from heaven, and using men as a plectrum sweeps across a harp or lyre (*The Exhortation to the Gentiles,* 8). Theophilus of Antioch speaks of the prophets "who became the instruments of God" (*To Autolycus,* 2.9). Clement of Alexandria speaks of the sacred writers as becoming "the organs of the divine voice" (*Stromateis,* 6.18). Macarius said that, just as the breath speaks by blowing through a flute, "so the Holy Spirit spoke through holy and Spirit-bearing men" (*Homilies,* 47.14). On this view the men who wrote the books of Scripture had no more to do with what they wrote than a pen has to do with an author's book, or a musical instrument has to do with a musician's music. All this would mean that the Bible is literally and, as it were physically, the word of God. For a variety of reasons it is not possible to hold this view.

Differences in the Biblical Text

There is first of all this simple fact. The early manuscripts were all copied by hand, and in the copying changes and errors crept in. It has been calculated that in the Greek manuscripts of the New Testament there are 150,000 places in which there are variant readings. True, sometimes it is only a difference in spelling, or a difference in the order of the words, or the substitute of one synonym for another. True, of the 150,000 fewer than 400 affect the sense, fewer than 50 are of any importance, and there is no case in which an article of faith or a precept of duty is left in doubt. This is perfectly true, but a reader would still have to decide which of the spellings, which of the variants is the word of God in the literal sense of the term. It might be said that what was the word of God was the first original manuscript as it left the hand of the original writer. If so, it is lost and gone for ever.

Take the case of the English text. In the late nineteenth century a committee of the American Bible Society examined six different editions of the Authorized Version, and they found nearly 24,000 differences. True, the variations made no material difference; but if a book is verbatim the word of God, then the words must be fixed, as well as the meaning, and in the case of the Bible this is simply not so. It would have been a strange thing for God to dictate the original work and then not to take equal care for its infallible transmission.

The Different Styles of Biblical Writers

There is the further fact that, whatever the biblical writers were, they were far more than pens in the hand of God, or instruments through which the Holy Spirit breathed. If this had been the case, we would have expected the Bible to be written in one level style the same all over. In point of fact every writer in the New Testament writes in his own style. If one who knows Greek well is confronted with a passage taken at random from the New Testament, and is asked to identify the writer, even if he or she does not know the passage, there will be no difficulty in saying whether it was written by Mark or Luke, by John or Peter, by the writer of the Letter to the Hebrews or by the John of the Revelation. In fact, the John of the Revelation often writes with such defiance of the ordinary rules of grammar and syntax that his style is unmistakable. His Greek is so bad that a modern schoolboy would get into bad trouble for writing it. There is no question of the suppression of the human personality. As G. E. Ladd has so well pointed out, the Bible is the word of God, but it is quite definitely in the words of men. The personality of the writers of the books of the Bible is certainly not obliterated. A pen and a musical instrument are things, but the biblical writers never ceased to be personalities in their own right.

Their independence is seen even in the way in which they tell a story. In the case of the story of the Gerasene demoniac, Matthew takes 7 verses to tell the story (Matthew 8:28-34); Mark takes 20 verses (Mark 5:1-20); Luke takes 14 verses (Luke 8:26-39). The Gospel writers are not men who are writing to divine or any other kind of dictation. In his writing each expresses his own personality and does things in his own way.

Variations Between the Four Gospels

Still further, there are the variations and the actual differences between Gospel and Gospel. In the first three Gospels the incident of the cleansing of the Temple comes at the end of the life of Jesus (Matthew 21:12, 13; Mark 11:15-17; Luke 18:45, 46); in the fourth Gospel it comes at the beginning of his ministry (John 2:13-17). Take the case of the different records of the same saying. It is often legitimately possible to explain differing versions of a saying of Jesus by saying that he repeated it in different versions on different occasions. But there are certain occasions which are quite definitely the same, and yet the recorded saying of Jesus, spoken on them, varies quite considerably. Take the case of the saying which comes after Caesarea Philippi and before the Transfiguration in all the first three Gospels:

> *Truly I tell you, there are some standing here who will not taste death before they see the Son of Man coming in his kingdom. (Matthew 16:28)*

> *Truly I tell you, there are some standing here who will not taste death until they see that the kingdom of God has come with power. (Mark 9:1)*

> *But truly I tell you, there are some standing here who will not taste death before they see the kingdom of God. (Luke 9:27)*

Unquestionably, we have here three versions of the same saying, and if the Gospels were written by divine dictation, surely there would not have been three versions of the one saying.

Take the case of Jesus' saying about himself at his trial, the saying which made his condemnation quite certain:

> *But Jesus was silent. Then the high priest said to him, "I put you under oath before the living God, tell us if you are the Christ, the Son of God." Jesus said to him, "You have said so. But I tell you,*

> > *From now on you will see the Son of Man*
> > *seated at the right hand of Power*
> > *and coming on the clouds of heaven." (Matthew 26:63, 64)*

> *But he [Jesus] was silent and did not answer. Again the high priest asked him, "Are you the Christ, the Son of the Blessed One?" Jesus said,*

> *"I am; and*
>> *'you will see the Son of Man*
>> *seated at the right hand of the Power,'*
>> *and 'coming with the clouds of heaven.'"* *(Mark 14:61, 62)*

> *They said, "If you are the Christ, tell us." He replied, "If I tell you, you will not believe; and if I question you, you will not answer. But from now on the Son of Man shall be seated at the right hand of the power of God." All of them asked, "Are you, then, the Son of God?" He said to them, "You say that I am."* *(Luke 22:67-70)*

Here are three different versions of the same saying on the same occasion. Divine dictation would not result in that.

One of the most surprising variations in the narratives of the Gospels is that the Gospels differ in regard to the time of Jesus' crucifixion. In the first three Gospels there is little doubt that the Last Supper is the Passover Feast (Matthew 26:17-20; Mark 14:12-17; Luke 22:7-14), and that therefore Jesus was crucified *after* the Passover. In the fourth Gospel, in John, there is no doubt at all that Jesus is said to have been crucified *before* the Passover Feast, for the Jews would not enter Pilate's judgment hall, in case they might be rendered unclean and so be disqualified from sharing in the Passover, and the day of the crucifixion is repeatedly called the day of preparation for the Passover (John 18:28; 19:31, 42). Further, in Mark the hour of the crucifixion is the third hour, 9 a.m., while in John the decision to crucify Jesus is not finally taken until the sixth hour, 12 o'clock midday. It is in the last degree improbable that divine dictation would have issued in a discrepancy like that.

Errors in the Gospels

On a very rare occasion there can be more than variation, there can be error. In the story of how the disciples plucked the ears of corn in the cornfield and so broke the Sabbath law, Mark makes Jesus remind the Pharisees of what David did in the days of Abiathar the high priest (Mark 2:26). Matthew and Luke both omit the name (Matthew 12:1-8; Luke 6:1-5). The priest in question was not Abiathar; he was Ahimelech (1 Samuel 21:1-6); Ahimelech was Abiathar's son (2

Samuel 8:17). The slip of a human mind is perfectly natural and completely unimportant, but such a slip is inconceivable in divine dictation.

Different Opinions Expressed in the Bible

There are occasions when students of Scripture have to exercise a judgment and a choice as to which of two parts of Scripture to follow. This is specially true in regard to Paul's teaching on marriage. In 1 Corinthians 7 Paul writes of marriage, and he is on the whole against marriage. If people are married, he does not want them to separate; if they are married they are to carry out to each other the duties and the obligations of marriage. But marriage for Paul, when he wrote that chapter, was a second best. It is well for a man not to touch a woman, but marriage is approved as a defense against the temptation to immorality (verses 1 and 2). It is better that people should remain unmarried. But, if they cannot exercise self-control, then they may marry, because it is better to marry than to be aflame with passion (verses 8 and 9). The whole attitude is that marriage is only justifiable when it saves a man from a worse fate! Why this attitude? Because Paul at this time was expecting the coming again of Jesus Christ at any moment, today, tomorrow, within weeks; he therefore wishes a man to have no distractions at all, and to concentrate on the coming end.

> *I want you to be free from anxieties. The unmarried man is anxious about the affairs of the Lord, how to please the Lord; but the married man is anxious about the affairs of the world, how to please his wife, and his interests are divided. And the unmarried woman and the virgin are anxious about the affairs of the Lord, so that they may be holy in body and spirit; but the married woman is anxious about the affairs of the world, how to please her husband. I say this … to promote unhindered devotion to the Lord. (1 Corinthians 7:32-35)*

Paul wrote this about AD 55; he is obsessed, as was the whole Church, with the idea of the coming of Christ. In view of that, marriage was a second best, one of the many things which might distract a man's attention from Christ in the brief time of waiting. But about eight years passed, and Paul wrote to the Ephesians. He knows now that he and his fellow Christians are living in a much more permanent situation, and in a great chapter he likens marriage to the relationship between Christ and his Church. A man leaves father and mother for his wife. It is "a great mystery." That is to say, it is the symbol of something splendid. Marriage is nothing less than the symbol of the relationship between Christ and his Church (Ephesians 5:21-33).

Now, if I am asked, What is Paul's teaching about marriage? where do I go to answer the question—1 Corinthians 7 or Ephesians 5? Surely to Ephesians 5, for any man has a right to be judged by his highest teaching. In 1 Corinthians 7 Paul actually says, "To the rest I say—I and not the Lord..." (1 Corinthians 7:12). Again he says, "I have no command of the Lord, but I give my opinion as one who by the Lord's mercy is trustworthy" (1 Corinthians 7:25). He is not writing to divine dictation here; he is giving his opinion. Over the years that opinion changed, and the Christian doctrine of marriage is not in 1 Corinthians 7 but in Ephesians 5.

The Bible as Inspired Revelation

We have now seen enough to realize that the conception of inspiration as producing a divinely dictated, infallible book produces far more problems than it solves. We must set out on some other course, and start all over again.

The Meeting Place of God and Man

If the Bible is the word of God, it must mean that in some way in the Bible a special connection is established between God and man. In some way in the Bible God and man meet. Man who is characteristically the seeker, and God who is characteristically the revealer, come together in this book. The Bible is uniquely the meeting place of the Spirit of God and the spirit of man. That is the first essential basis of any doctrine of revelation and inspiration.

Inspiration in the Human Situation

This means that the meaning of inspiration is to be found in the human situation, or, rather in the divine-human situation. It is in the connection established between the Spirit of God and the mind of man that the meaning of inspiration is to be found.

The Effects of Sin

So we have to ask, What is the human situation? The human situation has two elements in it. The first element is that man is the creation of God; but not only the creation of God; he is also made in the image of God (Genesis 1:27). This ought to mean, as Suzanne de Dietrich puts it, that "it is the vocation of man to live in a trustful relationship with God." To put it in another way, God is not only Creator; he is also Father. But now comes the second element in this human situation. It is essential for this situation that man must be born free. The relationship between man and God must be the product of a free invitation and a free response. To quote Suzanne de Dietrich again: "Man alone in all the creation can say 'yes' or 'no' to God." In point of fact, man has said "no." He uses his independence to take his own way. This is the very essence of the story of the Fall. He fails to see that his only real freedom, his only real self-fulfillment, must come from obedience to God. So man arrives at a situation in which he is travelling in the wrong direction, searching for happiness in the wrong place, looking for freedom where there is no freedom, and searching for fulfillment where there is no fulfillment. This is sin. The human situation is a situation in which man turns away from God to himself.

The Purpose of the Prophets

Because God is love, God has somehow or other to mend this situation. He cannot mend it by intervention from outside; he cannot intervene directly. This is so because the relationship between man and God must remain a free and spontaneous relationship, or it cannot be a relationship of love. It is therefore necessary that God should mend the human situation by human instruments. This is what he did—and the instruments he used to recall men to himself were the prophets.

Two things are to be remembered. A prophet was not so much a *fore-teller* of the future as a *forthteller* of the will and purpose of God. The great function of prophecy is not simply prediction; it is the proclamation of the will of God, and the announcement of the consequences, if the will of God is not obeyed. Further, prophecy was a much wider word for the Jew than it is for us. As we saw, when we were studying the making of the Old Testament, the historical books were called the former prophets. Moses was reckoned as a prophet; so law is prophetic. All Scripture is prophetic, for the prophet is the man who brings to his fellow men the voice of God. Now this is to say that the prophet is characteristically the link between God and man. This is his function; this is the reason for his existence. And, if the prophet is the man who establishes and restores the relationship between God and man, this is to say that the prophet *is* the man who speaks the word of God; the prophet *is* the inspired man.

The Characteristic of the Prophets

If this is so, we will have gone a long way to understanding the meaning of inspiration, the meaning of the idea of the word of God, if we can understand just what a prophet is. Suzanne de Dietrich points out two characteristics of the prophet.

- The prophet is the conscience of the nation. He is "the living conscience of the people at a moment when all other voices are silent."

- The prophet is under the absolute control of God.

    The lion has roared;
    who will not fear?
    The Lord GOD has spoken;
    who can but prophesy? (Amos 3:8)

- The prophet is the man who speaks because he must.

- The prophet is the man who in a special way has been in the inner council of God.

    Surely the Lord GOD does nothing, without revealing his secret to his servants the prophets. (Amos 3:7)

The prophet is not expressing an opinion or making a suggestion. The characteristic saying of the prophet is not, "I say," but, "Thus says the Lord." So, as Wheeler Robinson said, this is the difference between the Greek and the Hebrew. For the Greek, truth is something which is discovered by the searching mind of man; for the Hebrew, truth is something which is revealed by the Spirit of God. The typical Hebrew statement is: "He has *told* you, O mortal, what is good" (Micah 6:8). Not, "You have been able to discover what is good," but, "God has shown you what is good." The prophet is therefore quite clearly a man who must listen before he speaks. The prophet is the man who listens, who understands, and who communicates. The prophet has only one function—to restore, to establish, to maintain, to develop the relationship between God and man. He is neither scientist nor historian. His whole function has to do with the relationship between God and man.

Prophets as Men Who Know God

We can now put this in another way—clearly the prophet must be the man who knows God. Otherwise he cannot even begin to be a prophet. When the church in which he was an eider was looking for a minister, Thomas Carlyle's father said: "What this church needs is a man who knows God other than at secondhand." The prophet knows God at first hand.

Prophets Love God

But immediately the question arises—what does it mean to know? First of all, there is all the difference between *knowing about* a person and *knowing* him. There are many great figures in the political and the social and the academic and the sporting world whom we know about, although we do not actually know them at all. But still further, the word *know* is a wide-stretching word. We know many people; we know their face, their voice, their name, their job, their life story. We speak to them when we meet them; we pass the time of day with them. But how many people do we really *know*? How many people are there into whose mind and heart we can enter with sympathy and understanding, so that we know what they are thinking and feeling? That kind of knowledge depends on one further thing—it depends on love. For true knowledge there must be love. The prophet who is to bring the message of God must not only know God, he must also love God.

Prophets Obey God

But we must take a further step. To love is necessarily to obey. The proof of love is obedience. "You are my friends," Jesus said, "if you do what I command you" (John 15:14). Therefore the prophet is the man who obeys God. There is a moral element in inspiration. Those who see God are pure in heart (Matthew 5:8). The man who receives the blessing has clean hands and a pure heart (Psalm 24:4, 5).

We are now coming near a definition, which takes us half-way to our goal:

> *An inspired book, a book which is the word of God, is a book which effects a connection between God and man, thereby correcting the human situation, which has gone wrong. It is written by a man who knows God, because he loves God, and whose love has issued in an obedience which fits him to be the instrument of God.*

But we have not yet finished, because there is another line which joins up with this one. For a Jew the revelation of God was not a revelation in words at all; it was a revelation in events. For a Jew the great revelation of God is the history of Israel as interpreted by prophets, especially the deliverance from Egypt. Anyone who reads the prophets must see that a very large part of the words of the prophets consists in the interpretation of historical events. The prophet sees God's hand revealed in the event; he sees in the event what God has done, and what God is meaning to say.

We can therefore say with complete certainty that the revelation which God gives is given in action and event; and that the Bible is rather the record and the interpretation of these events than revelation in itself. The Bible is the story of God acting and men interpreting, or failing to interpret, the action of God. And now we come to the peak of the whole matter.

The supreme event is Jesus Christ. It is he who is the Word. The word is no written page. God's words are events; God speaks in events. And therefore the supreme event, the supreme revelation, the supreme word is Jesus Christ.

The Bible tells of the *preparation* for his coming in the Old Testament; it tells of the *event* of his coming in the Gospels; it tells of the *result* of his coming in the Acts; it tells of the *interpretations* of his coming in the Letters. The correct way to read the Bible is to begin in the middle with the saving event of Jesus Christ; then to go back to the preparation, and then on to the story of the Church, and the interpretations of him.

The supreme importance of the Bible is that in it and nowhere else we find Jesus Christ. Without it we would have no record of either the life or the teaching of Jesus. It may be claimed that even without the Bible we would have the tradition of the Church; but it is the Bible which prevents the distortion of that tradition. It is the touchstone; it is the assurance that no man can pervert the facts or invent new facts, for Jesus Christ is there.

I believe that the Bible is the word of God because in it alone we confront him who was uniquely the Word of God. So we come back to the great Reformation principle, the word of Luther: "The true touchstone for testing any book is to discover whether it emphasizes the prominence of Christ or not... What does not teach Christ is not apostolic, not even if taught by Peter or Paul. On the other hand what does preach Christ is apostolic, even if it should come from Judas, Annas, Herod or Pilate."

Here is the simple test—the Bible is the word of God because through it we find Jesus Christ.

So then finally we may sum up our conclusions:

• The Bible is the word of God, because it is the place where the broken relationship between man and God is repaired.

• The Bible is the word of God, because it was written by men who knew God, because they loved him and obeyed him.

• The Bible is the word of God, because it tells of the self-revealing, saving acts of God, culminating in the event of Jesus Christ.

• The Bible is the word of God because in it and in it alone we are confronted with the life and teaching of Jesus Christ.

Aids to Reading

Commentaries

The New Interpreter's Bible (Abingdon Press), a completely new commentary in twelve volumes, continues the tradition established by its predecessor, *The Interpreter's Bible.* Each volume includes two complete translations of selected books of the Bible; a detailed, critical commentary; visual aids; and reflections.

The Daily Study Bible (Westminster John Knox) consists of the New Testament devotional commentaries by William Barclay. Since his death a team of scholars has begun to produce similar commentaries on the Old Testament, with great success.

The Tyndale Commentaries (Inter-Varsity Press). These commentaries are written by conservative evangelicals, and are consistently valuable.

The New Century Bible (Eerdmans in the USA and Marshall Pickering in Britain). A fuller commentary both for introduction and for explanation of the text.

Black's New Testament Commentaries (A. and C. Black: in the USA *Harper's New Testament Commentaries,* Harper and Row). An advanced series, most valuable.

Hermeneia is a series published by Fortress Press in the USA and SPCK in Britain. It also includes translations from the German

Biblischer Kommentar series. It is a very advanced, and technical, series.

Word Biblical Commentaries (Word Books, Waco, Texas). A massive, up-to-date series on the whole Bible on the Hebrew and Greek text, from an evangelical standpoint. Very valuable.

A new one-volume commentary is desperately needed. The second edition of *Peake's Commentary on the Bible* is now nearly thirty years old. The most recent such work is the Roman Catholic *New Jerome Biblical Commentary.*

Bible Atlases

A good atlas is an important aid to reading the Bible. An excellent edition for study is the *Oxford Bible Atlas,* 3rd edn. (edited by John Day). A lavishly illustrated atlas which is geographical in approach is J. Rogerson's *Atlas of the Bible* (Phaidon, Oxford).

General Introductions to Studying the Bible

J. Rogerson (ed.), *Beginning Old Testament Study* (SPCK). Contains essays specially designed for college students beginning to study the Old Testament.

B. D. Chilton, *Beginning New Testament Study* (SPCK). Is the New Testament equivalent of the above.

Richard Coggins, *Introducing the Old Testament* (Oxford). Is an excellent and up-to-date book that introduces readers to the new methods that are being applied to the Bible.

Literary Approaches to the Bible

R. Alter and F. Kermode (eds.), *The Literary Guide to the Bible* (Collins).

Adele Berlin, *Poetics and Interpretation of Biblical Narrative* (Sheffield Academic Press).

Daily Bible Reading

Ellsworth Kalas, *The Grand Sweep* (Abingdon Press).

Maps

PERSIA

• Persepolis

Persian Gulf

ELAM

ARABIAN
DESERT

MEDIA

Susa •

ASSYRIA

Nineveh •

• Ur

Euphrates River

Red Sea

Asshur •

BABYLONIA

Babylon •

Tigris River

Haran •

SYRIA

• Damascus

Sidon •
Tyre •

Samaria
• Shechem
• Jerusalem

• Hebron

SINAI

• Thebes

HITTITE
EMPIRE

EGYPT

• Memphis

MACEDONIA

Mediterranean Sea

LIBYA

**THE ANCIENT
NEAR EAST**

Persian Empire
c. 500 BCE

Babylonian Empire
c. 560 BCE

Assyrian Empire
c. 640 BCE

SCALE OF MILES

0   50 100   200   300

Adapted from *Bible Teacher Kit*, Copyright © 1994 by Abingdon Press.

THE ANCIENT NEAR
EAST BEFORE THE
EXODUS

– – – – Abraham's Journey

SCALE OF MILES

0   50   100   200   300

Adapted from *Bible Teacher Kit*, Copyright © 1994 by Abingdon Press.

172

THE EXODUS

Traditional Route of the Exodus —·—·—

Possible Alternative Routes ·····

SCALE OF MILES

0   25   50   75

ISRAEL IN CANAAN
Joshua to Samuel and Saul

▲ Cities of Refuge
■ Philistine Cities

SCALE OF MILES

0 5 10 15 20 25 30

The Great Sea

Sidon

MT. HERMON ● Damascus

Dan (Laish)

Tyre

ASHER ▲Kadesh DAN

Hazor

BASHAN

ZEBULUN

NAPHTALI

Sea of Chinnereth ● Golan

MT. TABOR

ISSACHAR

Megiddo ● MANASSEH

MANASSEH ▲Ramoth-gilead

HILL COUNTRY OF ISRAEL

▲Shechem

River Jordan

THE ARABAH

MT. GERIZIM

EPHRAIM GAD GILEAD

Shiloh ● AMMON

Bethel ●
●Ai

Jericho ● Shittim
●
MT. PISGAH ▲Bezer

BENJAMIN

Jerusalem ●

Sea of the Arabah (Salt Sea)

Ashdod ■
Ashkelon ■ PHILISTINES

HILL COUNTRY OF JUDAH

Gaza ■

Lachish ● REUBEN

Hebron ▲ ●Aroer

River Arnon

JUDAH

●Debir

MOAB

●Beer-sheba

SIMEON

The Negeb

EDOM

The Great Sea

Gebal

PHOENICIA

Sidon

Damascus

SYRIAN
DESERT

Tyre

Dan

ARAM

Hazar

Mt. Carmel

Megiddo

ISRAEL

AMMON

Joppa

Beth-horon

Bethel

Jerusalem

Ashdod

Gezer

Jericho

PHILISTIA

Gaza

Hebron

Raphia

JUDAH

MOAB

Beer-sheba

EDOM

THE UNITED MONARCHY

■ Places fortified by Solomon

— Greatest extent of the empire

Territory conquered by David

Area occupied by Saul

Ezion-geber

Gulf of Aqabah

The following text appears within the map image:

HITTITES

Ugarit

KITTIM
(Cyprus)

Hamath

Arvad

The
Great
Sea

Gebal

PHOENICIA

Sidon

Damascus

SYRIAN
DESERT

Tyre

Dan

Mt. Carmel

Megiddo

ISRAEL

AMMON

Joppa
PHILISTIA
Ashdod

Bethel
Jerusalem
Jericho

N

W   E

S

Gaza

Hebron

Raphia

JUDAH

Beer-sheba

MOAB

EDOM

**THE KINGDOM OF
DAVID AND SOLOMON**

Greatest extent of
the empire

Territory conquered
by David

Territory under economic
influence of Solomon

Ezion-geber

THE
KINGDOMS
OF ISRAEL
AND JUDAH

SCALE OF MILES

0   10   20   30   40

Damascus

Sidon

KINGDOM OF
DAMASCUS

Tyre

Dan

PHOENICIA

ISRAEL

SAMARIA

River Jordan

The
Great
Sea

Joppa

Bethel

AMMON

JERUSALEM

Tokea

Moresheth

Lake Asphaltitis
(Dead Sea)

Gaza

PHILISTIA

Beersheba

JUDAH

MOAB

Kadesh-
barnea

EDOM

Arabian Desert

KINGDOM OF
EGYPT

Elath

N

W   E

S

Adapted from *Tear-off Bible Map Series*, Copyright © 1991 by Abingdon Press.

Sidon

PHOENICIA

ABILENE

Tyre

MT. HERMON

Caesarea
Philippi

PANEAS

ITURAEA

TRACHONITIS

Lake Semechonitis

ULATHA

BATANAEA

GALILEE

Capernaum

GAULANITIS

Sea of Galilee

Bethsaida
Julias

Cana

AURANITIS

Nazareth

MT. TABOR

Mediterranean Sea

MT. CARMEL

DECAPOLIS

Caesarea

MT. GERIZIM

SAMARIA

PEREA

Joppa

Jericho

JERUSALEM

Bethlehem

Bethany

JUDEA

Lake Asphaltitis
(Dead Sea)

Gaza

IDUMEA

N A B A T A E A

**PALESTINE
AT THE TIME
OF JESUS**

N
W E
S

SCALE OF MILES

0 5 10 15 20 25 30

To Samaria

N
W **E**
S

JERUSALEM
AT THE TIME
OF JESUS

Pool of
Bethesda

Fortress
Antonia

Location of
Jesus' Trial

Gethsemane

to Emmaus

Traditional
Golgotha

Via
Dolorosa

THE
TEMPLE

Bridge

Hasmonean
Palace

Palace of
Herod

UPPER
CITY

House of
Caiaphas?

LOWER
CITY

to Bethany

Upper
Room?

Pool of
Siloam

To Bethlehem

THE MINISTRY OF JESUS

Later Ministry of Jesus

SCALE OF MILES
0 5 10 15 20 25 30

Sidon

Mt. Hermon

Sarepta

Tyre

Caesarea Philippi

Gischala

Capernaum

Bethsaida-Julias

Magadan

SEA OF GALILEE

GALILEE

Mt. Tabor

Abila

Gadara

Caesarea

Ginae

SAMARIA

GALILEAN MINISTRY

Capernaum   Bethsaida-Julias

Cana   Gennesaret

Nazareth   Magadan

Ephraim

Philadelphia

JERUSALEM   Jericho

SEA OF GALILEE

Bethany

Nain   Bethlehem

Dead Sea

N
W   E
S

JUDEA

Adapted from *Tear-off Bible Map Series*, Copyright © 1991 by Abingdon Press.

PAUL'S
FIRST JOURNEY
Acts 13:1-14:28

SCALE OF MILES

0   50 100   200   300

Adapted from *Tear-off Bible Map Series*, Copyright © 1991 by Abingdon Press.

181

PAUL'S
SECOND JOURNEY

Acts 15:36-18:22

SCALE OF MILES

0   50 100   200   300

PAUL'S THIRD JOURNEY

Acts 18:23–21:17

SCALE OF MILES

0   50   100   200   300

Black Sea

Adriatic Sea

ITALY
ROME

SICILY

Mediterranean Sea

CRETE

Aegean Sea

THRACE

MACEDONIA
Amphipolis
Thessalonica
Beroea
Philippi
Neapolis
Samothrace
Mitylene
Chios
Athens
Corinth
ACHAIA

Byzantium

BITHYNIA AND PONTUS

GALATIA

CAPPADOCIA

MYSIA
Adramyttium
Pergamum
Smyrna
LYDIA
Ephesus
Troas
Assos
Samos
Cos
Rhodes

PHRYGIA
Antioch
PISIDIA
LYCAONIA
Iconium
Lystra
Derbe
KINGDOM OF
ANTIOCHUS
AMPHYLIA
Perga
Attalia
LYCIA
Myra
Patara

CILICIA
Cilician Gates
Tarsus
Antioch

SYRIA
Sidon
Damascus
Tyre

CYPRUS
Salamis
Paphos

Ptolemais
Caesarea
Joppa
Jerusalem
JUDEA

EGYPT

Adapted from *Tear-off Bible Map Series*, Copyright © 1991 by Abingdon Press.

PAUL'S
VOYAGE TO ROME
Acts 27:1–28:16

SCALE OF MILES

0   50   100   200   300

Adapted from *Tear-off Bible Map Series*, Copyright © 1991 by Abingdon Press.

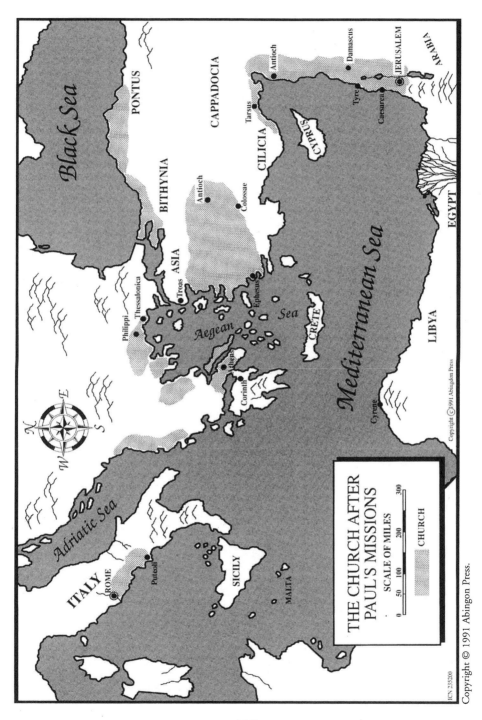

THE CHURCH AFTER PAUL'S MISSIONS

SCALE OF MILES

0   50   100   200   300

CHURCH

ICN 235200

185

Index